About the Author

Iestyn's early experience came touring with his country-and-western singer father, Terry Edwards. On variety bills, usually with a troupe of all-singing animal puppets, featuring Ernie Emu belting out 'Anything You Can Do I Can Do Better' and Jessie Giraffe taking her knickers off, four-year-old Iestyn would sing 'Please Help Me'.

Aged 12, Iestyn took up a Hammerstein Chantership at Southwark Cathedral, and later studied singing and piano at Guildhall. He created Madame Galina for Rag Week, and was promptly asked to leave the college. He sang seasons with British Youth Opera and gave recitals at Southwark Cathedral, Loseley Hall and the Chelsea Arts Club.

As Madame Galina he has appeared with Combined Services Entertainment on bases throughout Iraq and Afghanistan. He has also performed at the Royal Opera House Clore Studio, the Barbican, Café de Paris, the Tower Ballroom Blackpool, the Hippodrome Leicester Square and at other major theatres countrywide and abroad. He was twice runner-up in the London Cabaret Awards Best Speciality and Best Alternative act categories. He has been published in *The Times* and the *Mail on Sunday*. Joanna Lumley chose his recording of 'Tom Bowling' for her second *Desert Island Discs* programme.

GW00480930

Dear Tessa,,

MY TUTU WENT AWOL

Thank you so much!

love,

MY TUTU WENT AWOL

IESTYN EDWARDS

This edition first published in 2017

Unbound

6th Floor Mutual House, 70 Conduit Street, London W1S 2GF

www.unbound.com

ISBN (eBook):978-1-911586-26-5

ISBN (Paperback): 978-1-911586-06-7

Design by Mecob

Cover image:

© Shutterstock.com
© iStockphoto.com / Gary Blakeley

This book was produced using Pressbooks.com, and PDF rendering was done by PrinceXML.

I toured Iraq and Afghanistan with Combined Services Entertainment while I was living in South Villas, St Pancras. My landlord there was one of life's rare good people: Jeremy Byham. As Jeremy's tenants we were valued and supported. When I got home from Iraq after the first tour, there was a note from him: 'I think I've put two and two together and realised where you've actually just been. Ring my bell the minute you're back safe, please.' He gave me 'a little post-addendum' to my yearly tenants' Christmas hamper. Single malt has never since tasted as good.

This book is dedicated with much love, laughter and gratitude to the memory of Jeremy Byham.

Dear Reader,

The book you are holding came about in a rather different way to most others. It was funded directly by readers through a new website: Unbound.

Unbound is the creation of three writers. We started the company because we believed there had to be a better deal for both writers and readers. On the Unbound website, authors share the ideas for the books they want to write directly with readers. If enough of you support the book by pledging for it in advance, we produce a beautifully bound special subscribers' edition and distribute a regular edition and e-book wherever books are sold, in shops and online.

This new way of publishing is actually a very old idea (Samuel Johnson funded his dictionary this way). We're just using the Internet to build each writer a network of patrons. Here, in the front (and back) of this book, you'll find the names of all the people who made it happen.

Publishing in this way means readers are no longer just passive consumers of the books they buy, and authors are free to write the books they really want. They get a much fairer return too: half the profits their books generate, rather than a tiny percentage of the cover price.

If you're not yet a subscriber, we hope that you'll want to join our publishing revolution and have your name listed in one of our books in the future. To get you started, here is a £5 discount on your first pledge. Just visit unbound.com, make your pledge and type GALINA in the promo code box when you check out.

Thank you for your support,

Dan, Justin and John
Founders, Unbound

Super Patrons

Danik Abishev
Denzil Bailey
Joanna Barlow
Gavin Battle
Felicity Bissett
Vivacity Bliss
Tom Brent
Guy Burden
Jeremy Byham
Paul Carr
Robert Conway
Adam Cooper
Ruth Crow
June Douglass
Rupert Durrant
Terry Edwards
Petter Eneman
Jane Farquharson
Rupert Farquharson
Denise Farrell
Mairead Farrell
Michaeljon Fosker
Jillian George-Lewis
Julia Gooding
Kd Grace
Tom Gravett
Bridget Greensitt
Irish Grey
William Hackett-Jones
Eunhee Hackman
Gareth Hagger-Johnson

Angus Hamilton
Ben Harrold
Cynthia Harvey
Martin Harvey
Magnus Hastings
Sam Hayes
Harry Hepple
Fernanda Herford
James Hodgson
HoneyCabaret.co.uk
Steven Horsley
Anna Hulagan
Tony James-Andersson
Phill Jameson
Paul Jobson
Adam Kay
Marie Kearney
Crispin Kelly
Emma Kettle
Dan Kieran
Celia Leggett
Beric Livingstone
lizzieroper lizzieroper
Miranda Llewellyn
Megan Lloyd Stevens
Bruce Marriott
Auriol Marson
Liz Martinez
Robert Mawson
Eileen McCourt
Barry McGinness
Susie Medland
Daniel Millis
John Mitchinson
Maggie Morgan

Kate Napier
Colin and Kim Noble
Sergiu Pobereznic
Justin Pollard
Elizabeth Purves
Annabel Pyke
Leisa Rea
Kate Reiss
Mark Richards
Amy Rixon
Sorcha Rogers
Nick Rucker
Adam Skinner
Brian Snow
Nicki Spencer
Roger Staff
Simon Steer
Suki Stephens
Mervyn Stutter
Laurie Taylor
Simon Thomas
Vanessa Toulmin
Oliver Turner
Fred Turner
Olivia Walter
Kasia Watson
Luke Whittaker
Ralph Woodward

Prologue

I was outside the Camp Bastion NAAFI in my tutu. A nurse walked across to me over the petrol-soaked gravel, arms folded.

Oh God, no…

'It's about the casualties,' she said, gently. 'One of them was your mate, Stacks.'

Part One

Chapter One

'Why are you two so late? Read your itinerary. Her Majesty's only on between 7.03 and 9.46.'

'Someone wanted to shoot us,' I answered, breasting the top of the gangplank.

'Where?'

'In the overspill car park.'

'Is your singing that bad?'

According to my itinerary, this unwelcoming committee must be the Royal Marine called Stacks. He was in regimental dress, six two, baby of face, blue of eye and rocky of outcrop. A scar ran from his nose to his top lip. The itinerary said that Stacks was from a musical family and would provide sympathetic liaison.

'Bloody civilians,' he muttered, moving aside to let Louisa and I onto the main deck of the *Victory*. Then he ducked through the doorway to bring Louisa's harp on board.

The ship looked squat and tremendous. Filigree rigging, lines of flags to the sky, butterscotch prow and the late evening light reflected in the doll's-house windows. A band played 'Shenandoah'. An unlit beacon awaited the Royal Match.

Would Her Majesty have her own Swan Vestas, I wondered? No, probably the longer Cook's Matches.

Stacks was checking the itinerary: T200 Celebrations. The Royal Naval event marking the two hundredth anniversary of the Battle of Trafalgar. His copy was dog-eared, covered in scribbles and had clearly been folded in eighths.

To keep down his pants?

'Harp, deployment of?' he wondered. 'Ah! Have harp, will trundle. With me. And really: with me. Or I *will* shoot you.'

I remembered the smell on board from school outings: Lapsang

Souchong. I caught also beeswax, meat roasting, vinegar and spice. The vinegar and spice, along with the damp, were an asthma attack waiting to happen, and I told myself not to take overly deep breaths while singing. Under gleaming wooden beams hung with oil lamps, waiters in livery were arranging balloon brandy glasses on tables, laid out in two rows from the main doorway down to the museum-piece cots.

'When a sailor died,' I told Louisa, 'he was laid out in his cot with the curtains drawn. Before his sea burial, in case he might be malingering, an officer would sew through the curtain and in and out of the sailor's nose. Our sewing mistress, Miss Clossick, told us that, and made Sandra Betsina wet herself in the infants. Oh, and they used to paint the floor of the surgeon's quarters red to camouflage the blood.'

Stacks cut in. 'That's apocryphal.'

Clever bollocks. 'Somebody's been at the Discovery Channel.'

I was saved by two sailors in bell-bottoms honing in on the harp.

'We're to help you carry this piece of kit up to the Great Cabin,' said one.

Louisa followed them, a steadying hand on the harp as she went.

They still managed to prang a cannon. 'Sorry, ma'am. We were doing Semtex while the rest of them did harp transporting.'

A chef passed carrying a model of the *Victory* made from chocolate.

'Eyes front, mate,' he told me. 'Going to the Great Cabin and then in a padlocked fridge.'

Sir Alan West, First Sea Lord, in full gold piping and brocade dinner dress, loomed in a corridor.

'Sir,' said Stacks.

'Iestyn, well met,' said Sir Alan. 'Was getting rather anxious.'

Stacks said, 'Nearly didn't make it at all, sir. Tried to drive past a checkpoint. Cooper had knelt to shoot.'

'Apologies, Sir Alan,' I said. 'Traffic jam like at a hedge funders' post-crash bring-and-buy.'

'In excellent voice tonight, I trust?' Sir Alan was nodding, though I hadn't agreed. 'As we discussed, please no off-colour remarks in front of Her Majesty. Stacks will escort you up to the Great Cabin. He's highly decorated. Being deployed to Iraq in November.'

'Is that a threat?' I asked.

Sighing, Sir Alan said, 'First heard Iestyn sing at the Whitebait Supper last year. In the Trafalgar Tavern. Introducing his songs, he came out with a couple of real blush-inducers. Though, as you see him tonight, at least he was dressed down for the occasion.' Looking around, he added quietly: 'On certain *other* nights he's to be seen in drag in tutu and tights as his alter ego, Madame Galina, Ballet Star Galactica.'

That's me as a Russian ballerina on an international tour. My official dance partner is off and I replace him with someone press-ganged from the audience. The *Liverpool Post* said I had to be the result of a drunken one-night stand between Captain Mainwaring and Anna Pavlova.

'Comes on in the full ballerina get-up, horrendous make-up and knickers, trailing clouds of talcum powder,' Sir Alan continued. 'A review we read said how Madame would be as much at home in a dominatrix's dungeon as backstage at the Bolshoi. You can imagine how assiduous we've been at Admiralty House, keeping that kind of detail away from *Yachting World* and the *Mail on Sunday* Diary. I'm stumped, truly, as to how one would think up an act like that.'

I said, 'My Nana Atkinson had my baby photographs retouched at Boots in Bargoed. My dark, straight hair turned blond and curly, my white christening gown turquoise with an added empire waist. And I was no longer barefoot, but wearing ankle socks and fluffy pink mules. Nana Atkinson had made me look exactly as she did in her summer bingo-playing best. It was only a matter of time before, just for starters, I was in the school production of *Grease*, singing "Summer Nights" opposite Steven Harper.'

'Like Severina,' Sir Alan commented. 'Our steward. Real name's Steven. Serves behind the bar in drag alternate Thursdays. You ring the bell for gin and he appears in something a little too comfortable, frankly, with bits pencilled left, right and centre. Said he got his penchant for drag from playing Mabel in the Heads House production of *Pirates of Penzance*. At an all boys' public school someone has to play a girl.'

'Yes, except I played Sandra Dee in a mixed-sex comprehensive in Kennington. At age 12, I was the only pupil available with both the high notes for "Hopelessly Devoted" and the cleavage for "You're the One That I Want".'

Sir Alan gave Stacks a resigned look, then took a stopwatch out of his dress trousers. 'They've had what my wife insists are the six minutes needed for nose-powdering.' He pointed to his right as he moved off down the corridor. 'There are some sandwiches in the bar. Oh, Iestyn – my wife sends her love and says to break a leg.'

I had sat next to Lady Rosie at the Whitebait Supper. When the arrangements were being finalised for me to sing on *Victory*, I had hoped she would be on board.

'Oh no, darling,' she had said. 'I tend not to go to these naval bashes with my husband. He and his cronies are *so* clubbable; when they get together they cry, and the last thing they want is a woman being cynical all over the proceedings.'

Louisa was in the bar being served coffee by someone who I supposed must be Severina/Steven – in uniform, so this mustn't be an alternate Thursday. A sign beside him said not to help oneself to anything without official leave. I thought of asking officiously for a verse of 'Poor Wandering One' but instead I ordered a brandy, mainly for the sake of the balloon glass. It came in a beaker. The royal bodyguards, sitting at a table set out with silver tureens of sandwiches, watched *The Simpsons*. When Stacks said it was time, Louisa pried her hands away from a radiator, put on mittens and we followed him back along the top end of the banqueting area.

'Louisa, don't point your harp at the Queen,' I said. Stacks didn't rise.

On a table outside the Great Cabin was the sheer hulk of the chocolate *Victory*. I helped myself to a cannonball, passed one to Louisa and offered another to Stacks, who refused it.

'Of course you know not to address Her Majesty unless she addresses you first?' he said. 'Then it's "Your Majesty" all the way. Same goes for His Royal Highness, except then it's "Your Royal Highness" first off, then "Sir, Sir, Sir".'

'I know,' I said, remembering Kenneth Pemberton at Southwark Cathedral after we choir trebles had been given an identical briefing prior to meeting Princess Alexandra. The Princess had asked Kenneth if he had watched Denis Healey on TV the night before. Kenneth had answered, 'Yes, Your Royal Highness, Ma'am, Ma'am, Ma'am.'

Louisa said, 'Iestyn and I performed with Prince Philip last year.'

'You mean *for* him,' Stacks corrected.

I wondered if speaking out of the corner of his mouth like that saved him the use of a vocal cord.

'No, *with*,' I said. 'He was on the bill for one of the evenings at the Trafalgar Tavern. Lou and I performed sea songs and he read poetry. It was just after his best mate had died. The one that the Queen disapproved of, apparently, after the official dinner when he booby-trapped the royal chair with a whoopee cushion.'

Stacks, impassive, said, 'Perhaps don't bring that up.'

I asked him, 'Are you nervous about Iraq?'

'Are you nervous about singing tonight?'

'No, it's a thing I do.'

'Well, then.'

Reflected candlelight gleamed in cut-glass, silver and mahogany, in Her Majesty's jewels and in Sir Alan's medals. Beyond the dinner table stood a mannequin dressed in one of Nelson's uniform jackets. I was taken aback at how small it was.

Prince Philip commented, 'Oh, it's *him*'. Her Majesty looked quite sharply across the table at him.

Starting 'Tom Bowling' with full wellie, I heard my voice come back to me from the walls of the cabin and the corridor outside and reined it in. I looked around the table slowly as I sang, not letting my glance rest on anyone for more than a second or two. Whenever I looked at Her Majesty, she was watching me. Sir Alan was glued to his stopwatch.

'Oh, what a sad song,' said Her Majesty, starting to applaud.

I wished she would take off her gloves: they were deadening the sound of her clapping.

Sir Alan, still no tears, announced that Louisa and I would perform *The Death of Nelson*. 'But, Iestyn, we're running late...'

All right, all right: I've explained about the near shooting...

'... and Her Majesty must be off at 9.42 to catch the royal train...'

Surely Her Majesty can chuck the wrong type of leaves on her own track to delay her own train...?

'... so can you please cut a verse from it?'

I started to argue that it wasn't a Gilbert and Sullivan patter song. Louisa plucked straight into the opening bars.

O'er Nelson's tomb, with silent grief oppressed,
Britannia mourns her hero, now at rest...

Louisa and I walked the harp back to the car. The band was playing 'Abide with Me'. St John Ambulance volunteers were removing their on-duty armbands, no doubt sulking about the lack of respiratory failures, serious blood loss and fractures protruding through skin. I hoped the fire brigade were on their way to douse the beacon.

Louisa said, 'You realise you cut the wrong verse, so Nelson lived through Trafalgar?'

'Did I? I wondered why Sir Alan, Prince Philip and assorted naval cronies weren't having their clubbable cry.' I had a last look back at the ship. 'Quick! Trundle at the double, Lou. That Marine's on the gangplank. Probably wants me to walk it.'

Chapter Two

Her Majesty was pleased; Sir Alan was pleased – in spite of my snafu putting Nelson on operatic life support. I dreamt of performing in a new world of smart officers' messes, being toasted with balloon brandy glasses raised by blubbing brigadiers.

'Contact Nicky Ness at Combined Services Entertainment,' Sir Alan replied to my begging email. 'They deal with all things military and leisure. Request an audition. If you end up in Iraq, you might well see Stacks.'

Iraq indeed – try clubbable-crony cry-ins at The Connaught.

Walking to Nicky Ness's cubbyhole through the Combined Services Entertainment offices, I passed an emaciated man in his forties with a backward comb-over, bottle-green cords and an out-at-elbows tweed jacket.

'Loveliest of trees, the cherry now is hung with bloom along the bough,' he quoted. On his breast pocket was a badge: I ♥ Muswell Hill.

Once I was safely in her office, Nicky said, 'Insisted on an audition. Wants to raise morale with poetry. You've missed the burlesque girl bent on providing innocent delectation. And Muriel and Dolly from Lancing offering to sit.'

'For portraits?'

'Not sit *for* anything, just sit. In the Nissen hut, the NAAFI, by the parade ground. Providing a comfortable, maternal presence.'

Nicky was power-dressed in navy blue and had an immaculate peroxide-blonde bob. Her voice had a hint of a West-Country burr.

'Now, we're not rejecting your singing *per se*. Just we feel your Madame Galina act will be of more immediate use.' I nodded, as ever resigned to being my own warm-up act. 'I was in Edinburgh for your *pas de deux* with the leader of Plaid Cymru, but squaddies will be a whole different *corps de ballet*.'

I put on practice tutu and weekday tiara. As the crux of my act involves chivvying men out of the crowd to dance with, I had some misgivings when I saw that all the CSE PAs and archivists were women. As late in my warm-up as *ronds de jambes*, I still didn't have a back-up plan. Resigned to lesbianising my crux, I was giving them my 'Princess Aurora's Entrance', when Patrick, the Canon engineer, arrived to refill the photocopier toner…

'And then you come behind me for a partnered section of dance.' Patrick and I were at my crux; I was hoping the ink on his fingers wouldn't end up on my nice white tutu. 'Approach, approach, approach. Put hands just under floating ribs. No! Please keep thumbs flat and don't dig in with them – this is ballet, not S&M. Present me and await further instructions while I do thirty-two pirouettes. Don't I look marvellous doing them? Yes, thank you, I do. In a minute I am going to stop pirouettes. I'm going to run. I'm going to jump. And you're going to catch me…'

'You were like the Gorgon turning to clock the poor boy,' Nicky commented. Patrick was being taken off to the local pub for lunch on CSE, shocked and miming back strain. 'Thank God he could catch you. What do you do when the stooge isn't looking like a safe pair of hands?'

'Jump sideways and land at his feet in the arse position.'

'The lads will love seeing you make the officers do all that cavorting about. And it looks like you've enough gob on you, hopefully, to deal with Royal Marines if they get lairy.' She nodded briskly. 'I think we'll be having you. If you're game? You're right for our new format.'

Just then Combined Services Entertainment were putting together the comedy-club tour. Five stand-ups, self-contained, as little kit as possible, aimed at audiences numbering from 15 to 500. All the big noise, produced in a whisper: a tough squaddie crowd must feel the biggest impact from the smallest source.

I'd have gone with a desert caravan library…

And Nicky Ness wanted to add some juice. An idea, she said, had been simmering through her years presenting on Radio Gibraltar and attending CSE shows, before she ever knew that her current job existed.

Why not put drag on a military stage?

She sat me down at her desk. 'First thing to warn about: squaddies hunt as a pack.'

Like nuns.

'And they will turn as a pack. If that happens, it's not the time to grab the fire blanket off the wall and, without endangering yourself, try to do something about the fire – it's time to run.'

Surely not at a clubbable cronies' cry-in?

'Your security is of paramount importance to us, but we really can only guarantee it up to ninety per cent.'

If I end up being in the other ten per cent, neither of my parents must get my fur coat.

'You'll have to wear full body armour at all times.'

Won't I look just so butch…

'Under certain circumstances you will have to bed down with the squaddies.'

Wash your mouth out!

'Which is all I can tell you today. To quote the military themselves: it's now a case of hurrying up and waiting. We're given a window of opportunity and are expected quick sticks to bundle a show in through it.' She stood and we shook hands. 'It's not absolutely "stand by"; more a case of keeping tabs on your wet wipes and pan sticks.'

Er… what just happened?

Chapter Three

I was outside the Perranporth Post Office on 9 December 2005, in town to perform my one-man show. The promoter was Felicity, a neurotic in country casuals, court shoes and pillbox fascinator. In case of what she called 'protracted flurries' she had made me get to Perranporth by lunchtime for an eight o'clock show. She pronounced Cornish pasty Cornish *parsty*, and was so anxious that for some reason I mightn't actually make it to the venue (and she'd just had the upright Bechstein tuned on purpose) that she kept me where she could see me while she ran errands. To the church, the dry cleaners and the Citizen's Advice Bureau. I was listening to *The World at One* on the car radio. Saddam Hussein, in hiding, was refusing to attend his trial for crimes against humanity. (His exact location would be unknown for another week. In the meantime, Harold Pinter would accuse Bush and Blair of state terrorism; Bush would admit that the invasion of Iraq had been undertaken due to faulty intelligence and accept responsibility for the deaths of 30,000 Iraqis.) Suicide bombers had killed 27 trainee policemen in Baghdad, four American soldiers died in an IED explosion and 32 Iraqis were killed in a mortar attack on a bus.

I was watching a man in overalls and high-vis vest poking a pencil into a section of the Post Office's slate wall when my phone rang. 'Pan sticks and wipes at the ready...'

Ooh!

I had been hoping that Nicky Ness would ring. It was known on the circuit that Combined Services Entertainment paid well. And just then I was barely keeping myself in ballet flats, a full fridge and false eyelashes. True, I was cheap to run: peppercorn renting in what estate agents call 'sub-bijoux'; believing the most beautiful line of poetry in the English language to be 'Buy one, get one free'; spending winters in my bedsit dressed for an evacuation. But the wolf wasn't being kept from the bedsit door. It had moved in and was arguing the toss about floor plan dimensions, quoting Keats 'the tick of the deathwatch beetle', wafting the Farrow & Ball colour charts at me and saying it was thinking… Geometric Vermicelli to replace the 1960s' Lemon Mivvi.

'What's the gig?' I asked Nicky.

'Tour of Iraq.'

I blurted out, 'Where?' *You heard her.* 'When?' *I might just have time to go into hiding.* 'Why?' *I suggest she gets straight back on her rocker.*

I mean, obviously I knew that CSE took shows out to Iraq, but surely those were cage-fighting tournaments, Kevin Keegan with updated hair or page-three stunners with easily shucked burkas? Not me in a tutu, with my borderline hairy man boobs, oozing talc and…

… and what point of reference could the average squaddie possibly have for ballet? Surely waves of not caring would be the least shit reaction I could hope for? What if they didn't laugh? Or they threw things? Or sang the balletic equivalent of the derisive football chant? I had a vision of myself running into the Perranporth Post Office to interrupt Felicity buying designs-of-Marmite-jar-through-the-years commemorative stamps. 'Please, you must supportively and helpfully deal with this mad person on poor little me's behalf. Tell Nicky Ness I'm too busy with Cole Porter, anecdotes about scabies and mocking your raffle prizes to possibly think of going to Iraq.'

'Yes, Iraq,' Nicky replied. I sensed that she would be deciding something about my fitness or otherwise for the trip from my reactions. I must calm down. '*When* will be January the sixth. And as for *why*: it's because you'll be our secret weapon. As in, either the "wow" or the "what the f… ?" factor.'

All very well and good, but how had a banqueting room in Bond Street become a bivouac in Baghdad? 'And this would be just for the officers out there?' I clarified. 'We must remember that's what the First Sea Lord meant when he sent me to you.'

'There will be officers at the shows, but alongside all other ranks.'

Other ranks? I reminded her that I was drag...

(*Clever* drag, thank you: Shirley Van Zyl, a Johannesburg feminist commentator, called Madame Galina 'post-womanist vaudeville'.)

Whatever I might be, Nicky insisted that the boys were ready for it. Apparently, our boys loved dressing up. Even in the middle of a war zone, suggest fancy dress and there would be no problem with costume. Wigs, underwear, Lycra dresses – all packed away in the recesses of the bivvy bag. During a BBC report from Baghdad just after the invasion, there had been visible over the left shoulder of the British Commander being interviewed an impromptu performance of 'Hound Dog' given by a fully got-up Elvis. What more proof was needed?

I didn't want any proof at all, let alone *more*. Staring at that suddenly ominous section of slate wall in Perranporth, I wanted the whole idea of going to Iraq to bog off.

Nicky said, 'We're dealing with circumstances just clicking into place, hence the short notice. They've been having operational nightmares on the logistics front out there, but we so need to get something in for post-Christmas entertainment. It's lining up to be a dismal January out in theatre.' Really, they called war 'theatre'?

CSE had the pick of the current UK stand-up circuit and the dream four had said 'yes': Paul Tonkinson, Rhod Gilbert, Andy Askins and Gina Yashere. 'All geared up for all possible eventualities.'

I tried again, saying that by booking me, Nicky would surely be repeating the mistake of the Edwardian impresario who put Anna Pavlova with *The Dying Swan* on the same music-hall bill as a flea circus, a goldfish eater and Archie's Athletic Dogs.

'No, we need an act that will nail a final element of the show and make the audience take note in a way they've never had to before. As I say: the "wow" or the "what the f... ?" factor.' She paused. 'You might well see Stacks.'

Chapter Four

Aghast in my St Pancras bedsit on Boxing Day, I was googling photos of camel spiders. Nicky Ness had already warned me off 'surfing for insurgency', and I stopped watching the news after I saw footage of Ronald Schulz, an electrician working in Iraq, who was held hostage and later shot. Shortly before Christmas, Tony Blair made a surprise visit to Iraq, and I'd studied both terrain and squaddies behind his head during the television coverage. The terrain looked as dry and flat as the squaddies' reactions to seeing him. I paused a YouTube video of a mouse and a camel spider fighting in a bucket, and rang my dad to tell him I was going to perform in Iraq. He spluttered and dropped the phone. My stepmother came on the line.

'Iestyn, what on earth has happened?'

I told her.

'Oh, sweetheart, really? Oh, now look at your father…'

Her description of the eczema breaking out around his hairline made me think of a pomegranate in a microwave. I promised her that I would phone the second I was back safe on British soil.

When I rang my mother she said, 'I'll tell the Waterloo Action Centre old ladies. They can knit things for you to take out for the soldiers, like our mothers did in the Second World War.'

I said not to tell anybody else, as CSE had advised us to let our next of kin know that we were going to Iraq, but otherwise to keep the trip secret.

'Well, I'm sure this CSE lot know what they're doing. Follow what they tell you to the letter, I would. Just make sure you've got some home comforts out there with you. Like when I go to Egypt, I always take my own kettle, bedside lamp and the bath mat.'

My parents could never have reassured me; with CSE's rule about not talking to anyone other than next of kin, I would have to deal with my fears alone. By 4 January, I was starting to panic and rang my mate in the Royal Ballet, Tom Whitehead.

'I'm going to perform in Iraq.'

'As Galina? Do they give you a gun to protect yourself? When do you go?'

'Day after tomorrow.'

He was silent for a time. 'An experience like this will be a full-stop, new-paragraph scenario. Full-on decision to have made.' He wondered if the food would be shit, and would there be disease? 'How do you get out there? Do you get military escorts?' I explained about CSE. 'I'd never even thought about entertainment in Iraq, let alone the logistics of it getting there. Of course, you wouldn't just get a base's number from Iraq directory enquiries and ring them up saying to put the lights on ready round the dressing-room mirror.' He gave his smoker's laugh. 'Sex-starved squaddies: bonanza for you. Seriously, mate, be careful. I suppose you get dos and don'ts of staying out of harm's way: stick with them. And don't be shit onstage, or they'll have you.'

Tom had echoed something my mother had said: about following instructions and trusting those who knew what they were doing. Giving this trust might well turn out to be that hiding to nothing, but my breathing just then tended to be a gasp in and a sigh out, my face looked like red tapioca and I was hearing myself making a continual soft keening sound. I had no choice but to trust.

CSE Tour Info: Safety & Security:

> You will be required to wear combat body
> armour and helmets during travel in between
> locations and sometimes inside certain bases.
> You will be issued with body armour and
> helmets at Brize Norton and you will be
> responsible for it until you return to Brize
> Norton. As you will be expected to carry
> your own sets throughout the tour (they
> weigh around 8kg) and sleeping bags you are
> advised to pack as lightly as possible to avoid

having to carry too much weight in total. We
have found from experience that lots of bags
can be one hell of a trip hazard going down
the steps off the Tristar.

Clothing/Footwear to take away with you:

Should be suitable for all conditions. Some
essentials that you need are strong walking
boots, flip flops for shower, nightwear, towel
(or two), toiletries and basic medication such
as sun cream, insect repellent, painkillers,
throat sweets and disinfectant hand spray.
You are advised to speak to a pharmacist/GP
regarding anti-malarial medication (which
can be bought over the counter at pharmacies
and SSVC will reimburse you for any
medication purchased for this tour).

No mention of a sun hat, but I thought I would probably need one;
and the Household Stores was on the way to the chemist. I tried
on the hat with the widest brim. I looked ridiculous. Still, it might
make the squaddies laugh. Needing a free hand for my wallet at the
till, I put the hat on again. The shopkeeper laughed.

The possible side effects from taking anti-malarial tablets read
like schlock horror. I asked the pharmacist if I would really need
them.

'Where are you going?' He looked up from sorting asthma
inhalers.

'Iraq.'

'It won't be malaria season. But I hear beheadings are rife.'

Tactless much?

I decided that just for once I would eschew the reduced-for-
quick-sale shelf in Camden Sainsbury's. Tonight – who knew?
Might be my last ever meal. Musing on famous last words – 'Let not
poor Nelly starve'; 'How were the receipts today at Madison Square

Garden?'; 'Take a step forward, lads. It will be easier that way' – I fingered the Taste the Difference pâté, goujons and ganache.

Until the voice of Stop Being a Fucking Soprano whispered in my ear to just buy the usual baking potato as there would be food on base in Iraq.

With the potato in the Baby Belling (come again? As the oven only worked on full heat and the left hotplate had died, it was more a gleam in its father's eye), I took down my Christmas decorations and packed for Iraq: A5 block pads, pens, *Mansfield Park*, make-up, wet wipes, tiara, hairnets, ballet shoes, white ballet tights to dye in tea when I got to Basra and clothing to do me in all weather conditions from depths of Amazonian jungle to up Welsh mountain. (Forgetting the sun hat, as it turned out.) I wrote a cheque for the balance of my Santander account and enclosed it with a letter to my landlord: 'Dear Jeremy, Please make sure Tom Whitehead gets this money: his details above.' Marking the envelope, 'In Case the Marines/camel spiders/insurgents – delete as appropriate – get Poor Little Me', I taped it to the mirror. An early supper – and tanked on Rescue Remedy, so to bed.

The squaddies won't like my act.

And the award for Most Specious Understatement goes to...

They might chuck stuff.

The officers might chuck stuff!

When we went with Sunday School to Southsea that boy had an admiral's hat and had to phone his mum every day, and he took so long one day some people queuing up to use the phone started banging on the door. He opened the door and handed the phone over, saying his mother wanted to speak to whoever it was, then started sobbing really rackingly. Clearly already in training to be a crying clubbable naval crony.

Where would they get the stuff to chuck at me?

Prisoners sharpen toothbrushes, pens and toilet brushes into shanks.

I once wrote in a geography exam that Egypt bordered South Africa.

I can't stamp on camel spiders if I'm wearing sandals: they'd incarnadine my feet like Lady Macbeth's hands.

And what was the drill in case big stuff kicks off with the insurgents? 'Get under hard cover'?

In Penelope Fitzgerald's The Bookshop, *the schoolgirl helping with the library gets a black eye when she's fetching in the washing and a frozen blanket gets blown into her face.*

Chapter Five

Terror woke me from a doze at 4.37. The last time I'd been up so early was to prank-call Nana Mouskouri. I did ballet barre straight out of bed, holding onto the side of my Welsh dresser. A half-moon hung over The Lord Stanley. Mogatroyd, the black Persian mix, sprawled on the gatepost of number four opposite. Lights were on in number eight, showing the wall-to-wall and floor-to-ceiling oil paintings and, as I dipped forward, hand to shin, Bernard, in his usual tweed, reading in a wing chair. A van driver chanced his suspension against a speed bump and Bernard looked down into the street. I imagined that I could hear him tutting to himself now. Mogatroyd hadn't reacted. I was commanding myself to notice these small things to stave off the terror at the big thing.

When I left the house Mogatroyd was still on his gatepost, watching foxes painstakingly decorate the cobbles with the contents of black bags. I carried my wheelie case as far as the main road, then set it down to drag – 'Well begun is half done!' I texted CSE tour manager Ian to say I would be in Pembroke Gardens in an hour and a half as arranged. In the Inner Circle of Regent's Park, I realised that for quite some time I had been making my keening noise. About to cross beneath the Marylebone flyover I envied the driver of a Saab going to his architecture practice while I was going to a war zone. It started to drizzle when I turned into Pembroke Gardens.

'Is that you?' A text from Ian.

A black people carrier with tinted windows was double-parked. The passenger door slid open as I drew alongside.

'Nice day for it. Not.'

I stowed my hand luggage and slid into the passenger seat. Ian was fortysomething, balding and jowly, with a rasp in his voice. He was dressed in black combats, sweatshirt and puffa jacket. I sized him up for possible pressganging onstage for my act – he might be a little serious – then remembered that, anyway, an audience tends to think it's a set-up when you pick on your colleagues. Waiting staff at a corporate event, for example. Always a no-no. I was desperate once at Steam and Rye with just hens out front and used Ferenc, the Hungarian bar-back. He was pretty, willing to show off a beautiful torso; but he couldn't understand what I was asking him to do, I kept snagging my tutu on the juicer protruding from his BKD and when the *pas de deux* was in extremis he excused himself to replenish glasses, Arbequina olives and artisan breadsticks. Nothing like as bad as Kyle, the waiter at Olympia. The event was *My Sex, You Sex, We Sex.* Acts were forbidden to make physical contact with members of the public. Kyle was a boylesque performer who decided that my getting him onstage was an opportunity to further his career by stripping down to a chicken-feather G-string, singing 'The Gay Thou Madest Me, Lord, Rear-Ended' and… actually, the least said about his use for that martini glass the better.

So, no pressganging Ian then. Driving past the chalk-cliff tenements of Paddington, Ian said that part of his remit was to make sure I was at all times fully up to speed with what was happening as the tour progressed, so I mustn't take it personally that his instructions might seem basic and obvious. I told him not to worry, but to be as basic and obvious as he needed.

'One, Ian, my favourite non-fiction book is *Mastering the Art of French Cookery*. The instructions for tipping an omelette out of the pan onto a plate go on for four pages. And we're talking plain omelette. Not ham, cheese or Burgundian truffle. Two, I'm scared to death.'

Ian was nodding. 'The Royal Marine looking after us in Basra will likely be the same with the instructions. Actually, he'll be far worse. Any questions you need to ask?'

'Tell me about camel spiders.'

'Unlikely we'll come into contact with any. It's winter. And they'd only ever be running after you because they want to stand in your shadow in the heat.'

'So they're not going to jump on my face and start chewing as soon as we land?'

'Most unlikely.'

'And what reaction do you think my act will get from the squaddies?'

'You never know absolutely how anything will go down. They'll never have seen anything like you. But Nicky said *she* laughed. We're going to a variety of bases. What storms in one may nosedive in another and vice versa.'

All too soon we were passing jaundiced brick in rural Oxfordshire and I could see the Brize Norton airfield, looking a lot like Alcatraz, but minus the redeeming water feature. Into departures and Ian fetched two lots of body armour and metal helmets.

'Store this in the overhead locker on the Tristar and put it on when instructed to do so by the captain. He'll also tell the cabin crew at the same time to turn out all the lights in the cabin, and fly the plane down into Basra in full- on helter-skelter mode for evasion purposes.'

'Sounds fun.' I was keening internally as I hefted my way into the navy-blue weighted waistcoat of the civilian body armour. 'Why is there an iron bit over just the heart? My right lung needs protecting. I use it for singing. And I'm already borderline asthmatic.'

'Nada on that score, mate.

I asked 'Where's the Duty Free? I need to buy a metal Bible.'

As we sat in departures among squaddies in desert camouflage and bottle-green anoraks – why would they ever choose to be here and now on the way to do this Iraq malarkey? – Ian taught me to recognise the various insignia of the three armed-service branches and of the ranks within them. I excelled at this. 'And an RAF Squadron Leader is most clearly recognisable because on his tunic cuff can be found, squashed at the wrong angle, the lesser chosen Liquorice All-sort.'

In your inner space no one can hear you scream.

An hour or so before departure time, all turns and crew had mustered for the inaugural CSE Comedy Store tour. Nicky Ness, in beige fleece and tracksuit trousers, was awash with expectancy. 'I can't tell you how thrilled I am to have got you all for this tour. The five of you acts, plus Ian as my trusty heavy and Spoons pushing all the right technical buttons.'

Four of the turns – Paul 'Tonks' Tonkinson (compère), Andy Askins, Rhod Gilbert and Gina Yashere – were swapping shared Jongleurs and agents stories. The other – me – stood smiling my in-the-dentist's-chair-but-unafraid smile. Nicky put her arm round me – 'Got the jitters, hon?' – and led me away.

'Terrified. Primarily, that the squaddies will hate my act. But there'll be weird dangerous things flying about or tunnelling in the sand. And insurgents.'

'We're all jittery, hon. New one on us all, this format.'

'And they're all new on me, the others, Nicky, but all know each other from the stand-up circuit.'

She nodded. 'In all respects, right out of your comfort zone.'

'But my ultimate challenge of an audience.'

Perhaps this tour of Iraq was overdoing things the other way, but it hadn't been much of a challenge performing Madame Galina at the leaving do for an English National Ballet dancer. Or at the Flower Festival Supper for the Dean of Bocking. Or the Trondheim Hairdressers' Convention.

'Shadow Tonks and his notebook,' Nicky advised. 'See, he's off for a wander now. Pick up gen on larger-than-life squaddie person-alities to target for your *pas de deux*.'

She walked me back to the fold and I sat down next to Andy Askins. He had startling dark eyes setting off simian features. He finished sticking a My Name Label on a bedding roll. 'Just to get this out of the way early doors,' he said, 'I told my wife I was descended from Eskimos and she believed me.' He called over to Gina, 'What's in the comfort kit?'

Gina was clutching a large, see-through plastic bag.

'Travel cushion, socks, slippers, sleep mask,' she said. 'Things that go with me as soon as we start talking about a longer journey than the one-four-nine from the end of my road to Waitrose. Oh, and some real CSE tour essentials: iPod, Blackberry, Gameboy, *War and Peace* on Wii.'

So far, CSE seemed to be a friendly and, more importantly, sane company. But then on Christmas Eve I'd shared a variety bill with burlesquer Scatte Erkushen, singing 'Santa Baby' dressed as a toilet, Scottie the Human Femidom and the inevitable three drag queens dressed as Vixen, Blixen and Cupid, giving their rendition of 'Let It Snow' into three tunable copper buckets by way of synchronised pissing.

I introduced myself to Spoons, the CSE techie. He was mid-thirties, with a short quiff and features like a fleshy chisel.

'Can you please put as strong a light on me as you can?' I asked. 'To keep my tutu looking as white as possible for as long as possible out in the desert. I always need to be washed out with over-bright lighting.'

'So I can imagine,' he drawled.

'Ah, CSE, good to find you here. Callum Seckerson.'

Callum was short, squat and pasty. No use onstage as a warrior. Would be cast as comedy vicar, village squire murder victim or ship's steward inevitably left out of lifeboat. I tried to work out his rank from his insignia.

'Major,' he prompted, and turned to Nicky. 'It's a fine tradition, military entertainment, I always say.' He looked the type to be always saying something. 'The Japanese and the Germans have always taken prostitutes to their soldiers, whereas we have always taken out our very finest.'

Including some of my own entertainment heroes: Coward, Gielgud, McCormack, Novello and Fonteyn. Olivier and Richardson toured Shakespeare through Europe in 1945, while Grenfell toured North Africa, the Middle East and India in her one-woman shows, with bits falling off (and sometimes magically reappearing back on) various pianos. Coward, again, would be lampooned with Carmen Miranda and Marlene Dietrich in Peter Nichols's play *Privates on Parade*, based on Nichols's experiences of CSE shows in the Second World War. By the time I worked for it, CSE was the biggest booker of mainstream stand-up in the UK; its bands were quietly legendary. In 2010 CSE would pull off an A-lister coup, taking David Beckham out to Afghanistan.

'Our very finest,' Major Seckerson was agreeing with himself. 'And what have you selected from your illustrious stable to bring out to us this time?'

Nicky answered, 'Four stand-ups, a school-of-Victoria-Wood, Middlesbrough United nut who told his future wife he was an Eskimo – and she believed him – and Madame Galina, Ballet Star Galactica.'

'Which is?'

'Character comedy with advanced stooge work and classical ballet skills,' I answered.

The Major was trying to look *au fait*.

'Post-womanist vaudeville,' I added. 'A feminist commentator said so in the South African press.'

The major still wasn't getting it.

'Drag ballet.'

I will never trust my costume and make-up to an aeroplane's hold, so had tutu and tights etc. in a Primark bag to take on as hand luggage. I set off the security sensor. The duty officer waved me back. In RAF blue, his eyes were stern, his nose and cheeks dull grey and the texture of egg boxes. He would, I presumed, be staying put at Brize Norton and would thus be out of range for supporting pirouettes in Iraq. I gave him a carefully conceived frown – lifting cheekbones to meet descending temples, chin-dimple to the fore – to convey that I couldn't possibly be setting off an alarm: my loose change, keys and whatnot were just then bumping their way through the x-ray machine. And only fluffy things in here, look. I squeezed my Primark bag: 'Oodles of tulle.'

'CSE,' Nicky quickly explained.

The officer waved me forward again. Further beeps.

He joined me on the wrong side of the sensor, put his hand in the Primark bag and pulled out my Swan Queen tiara.

I said, 'I thought I should bring my most bells-and-whistles headpiece out to Iraq.'

Eyeballing first me, then Nicky and, lastly, the heavens, the officer waved me through. 'Find some other way to stow this rather specialised piece of kit.'

'Sir,' I said. He clearly thought I was being insubordinate. I wasn't. Half shielding me from him Nicky explained that I was new to this palaver and propelled me onward.

The runway at Brize Norton was, for some reason, out of order and we were now shown onto shuttle buses bound for its replacement.

Watching me try, and fail, to stow my Swan Queen tiara in my make-up bag, Nicky asked, 'Do you wear false eyelashes onstage as Madame Galina?'

'No, my real lashes are so long, I just put on some volumising mascara.'

A very young squaddie across the aisle turned to stare – no wings... no sword... no *tunic*, let alone squashed lesser chosen Liquorice Allsort – army private.

'Morning,' I said, reaching over to shake his hand. 'Are you going on the Trident with us?'

'Different,' he said, turning immediately away.

Couldn't get him onstage: whatever banter I tried to get going, he would strangle at birth.

Nicky reminded me yet again that on this tour I would be either the 'wow' or the 'what-the-f... ?' factor. 'And the plane we're going on isn't a Tri–dent, it's a Tri–*star*.'

Whatever, I was expecting at the very least *Thunderbird 2*.

And surely not that thing parked over there.

This was a 21st-century military excursion: we couldn't be going by Orville, the cartoon albatross?

We waited in a secondary departures building. With its halogen-lighted glass atrium and lurid green and blue check-in lanes it was like sitting in a vintage pinball machine. I stared balefully out at the runway. We were indeed going on Orville, the Cartoon albatross.

I hustled self, Primark bag and body armour to the top of the airstairs, where a flight attendant in a tan onesie (though there was definite stage potential in that chin) pointed me to the first-class cabin. 'VIPs, sir.'

He must surely have that wrong, but I thanked him and made a dash left.

I'd be first on board a flight to the *Twilight Zone*. Mustn't have other spinsters beating me to all the spare blankets, cushions, magazines and complementary items (where available) for their own in-seat enjoyment.

'Ooh, comfy!' I blurted out, sitting down. And though I might still be thinking that leather seats of this vintage ought to form a corner and be covered with zebra print, droppings from joss sticks and Jean Shrimpton's vinyl-booted thighs, I was relieved to be hearing from my inner Stop-Being-a-Fucking-Soprano voice. I spread out, put my body armour and helmet on the empty seat to my right and hugged my Primark bag.

'Not crowding you sitting here, I hope?' Ian said, taking the empty seat to my left. 'Just staying with you as it's your first one. And as the flight might well be full, maybe stow your body armour up there?'

I calculated the time it would take to put it on from where it was, and how long from the overhead locker. 'I'll put it under the seat in front.'

Sounding as though he was reciting from an official document, Ian asked, 'Also, remember, you must be certain that in the case of an incident you can lay hands on what you know at a glance to be your body armour and nobody else's.'

'I can. Look.' I showed Ian. 'The security officer did say to stow it a different way…'

I'd found a hook and loop on the side of my Kevlar helmet that might have been designed specifically to hold a Swan Queen tiara.

The flight attendants' *Two-doors-to-the-rear* ritual dance looked incongruous on such ripped builds and thousand-yard stares, but the pilot's announcement was reassuringly familiar – cruising speeds, altitude, weather on arrival.

Until he carelessly mentioned our destination. My Stop-Being-a-Fucking-Soprano voice was immediately shouted down.

Really, what am I doing?

Do I absolutely need the money from this excursion of outrageous silliness?

Yes, actually, I do – unless for some reason I missed my recent coronation as Queen of Sheba.

If I bail now, will I have to recompense CSE for any expenses already incurred on my behalf? Even Felicity, the promoter in Perranporth, reminded me that according to the terms of our contract, had I bailed on her, I would have been required to refund her for ticket printing, hire of the hall – and she didn't know how liable she might be having personally, and a great number of times, reassured that one punter that I would definitely be performing, so it would be worth his while to fly specially from Essex to Cornwall. (Yes, she was aware now that he was my cross-dressing Colchester stalker…) What have CSE paid out on my behalf to date? Shoestring fries with goats' cheese at the lunch the day they signed me. Ian's petrol money. Insurance cover in case of my death or serious injury.

Oh, and I've still got their magic marker issued to tag my body armour.

I'm getting off Orville, the cartoon albatross. I'll find Nicky and tell her that I've led her along and I'm sorry, but I really can't put myself through this.

Except Nicky's gone out on a limb for me. I'm her risk.

Yes, and I might well tank in Iraq, get canned off, reports will get back to the MoD. Nicky could get court–martialled.

All round for the best, I'll get off without her seeing me and make a run for it. Then I won't answer my phone for a fortnight and hope that in the meantime I and my inconvenience will simply have been forgotten.

Like when Jane Eyre tells St. John Rivers she won't become a missionary, thanks, then hears Mr Rochester call and without a by your leave rushes back to Thornfield. 'And his sight returned and his arm grew back and all was— '

'Shit!'

'Problem?' Ian wondered.

'The Tristar's taxiing.'

The flight attendant with the theatrical chin asked me, sir, to please strap myself in. 'And were you really expecting the Tristar to get airborne without taking its run-up?'

I didn't think I possibly could, but I slept until Ian woke me for food. There was a squaddie sitting in front of me now. He had sharp features placed well forward. Two more squaddies sat across the aisle to my right. The one in front put aside the goriest Nintendo war game (I know: but then, I watch a lot of ballet videos in my spare time) and asked for the chicken. He looked down as the meal tray was put in front of him, commented that the dead quota had gone seriously up some notches now, and gave the food trolley a once over. 'Don't suppose there'd be a miniature of Pinot Grigio?'

He was told that he supposed right.

Ian mouthed to me, 'Marine.'

Handsome, witty, had used irony – I leant forward in my seat to look through the gap. And, with those quads, definitely a potential Nijinsky to my Karsavina.

I ate my chicken, cubed root vegetables and mash, pre-packed cheese and biscuits, washed down with orange juice. I decided against the tub of something blancmange-like.

'Hoorah, nice,' I said, yet again thankful for food – before any digestion could actually have taken place – being so kindly restorative.

The Marine was leaning out of his seat and, I realised, checking for what others might leave uneaten. The two squaddies to our right didn't look up. For a few seconds he watched them. They looked more demonstratively down at their food trays, indicating that they would want all that they had.

'Mate,' I said.

He shifted to peer round his seat at me, seemed slightly confused, then looked down at my tray. 'Do you want this?' I asked, offering him the blancmange-like something.

'Please, fella,' he said, taking it from me. 'When they do the tea run you can have my custard creams.'

After a flight of six and a half hours, the pilot announced that we were entering Iraqi airspace and should put on body armour and helmets. Neither Ian nor the three squaddies needed to look anywhere but front to swiftly don their helmets. I needed to first unclip a Swan Queen tiara from mine, then couldn't find the label, lost a game of cat's cradle in reverse with the straps and dropped it on the floor. The Marine handed it back to me.

I need to look slicker doing all this militaristic manoeuvring.

Oh, sweet, the Marine's turned round to check I'm finally sorted.

I take it his revolving–index–fingers manoeuvre is to indicate that I have the helmet on back to front.

Maybe return the thumbs–up next time and don't waggle fingers at him like Miss Mapp.

Oh, come again, he's smirking: seems to like the finger-wagg—

Mayday! Mayday! Mayday!

Captain, for the love of all things, stop making Orville, the cartoon albatross, do up tiddly up up and down tiddly down down.

Fuck, it's a flak attack!

The wheels are biting.

Brace!

Brace!

We're saved, saved…

Why am I the only one applauding?

Ladies and gentlemen, welcome to Iraq. We hope you enjoyed your flight with us on Orville Airways. The weather on the ground is fine, with a mild wind coming in off the desert.

Any military personnel that are not yet equipped with a shank to lob at the drag ballerina should report immediately to the NAAFI.

Chapter Six

A strong smell of petrol, the bray of generators, squaddies hurrying in quilted body warmers. We crossed from the runway to a holding bay. Gina commented on the size of the squaddies' kitbags and the number of segments they comprised, wondering if they bought the bits as separates and put them together – like from a military IKEA.

Ian called out a warning about a trip hazard. I wondered (deranged) how an insurgent could have got in here with both bomb and wire detonator, but stopped dead, sensing myself go pale. Ian clarified, 'The trip hazard's the bottom of that door frame.'

The holding bay was a hangar which somehow managed to give two impressions simultaneously: the first of a new build with details still to be finished, the second of falling-down decrepitude. The Marine from the seat in front of me was in and among all the others just disembarked, wading through a stream of kitbags. Normally, I'd be rugby-tackling anything that was vaguely the same colour as my case, but here, in these circumstances, I thought I should hold back.

And why would anyone be in a hurry to get to the front line?

The Marine suddenly froze, peering down at the stream. He ducked and made a grab, then came up with a bag.

Nodding as he walked by me, he said, 'Get in there, mate. Won't bite you.'

'You all first,' I said. 'Priority, surely?'

He stood next to me facing the goings-on, shucked his kitbag and leant it against his knees. 'It is now twenty-one hundred hours. Transport won't be here till twenty-three hundred hours at the earliest expectation.' He turned slightly and put out his hand. 'Charlie. Should have introduced myself before I took your pudding. Don't take that the wrong way.'

'Iestyn. I won't. If you'll be delayed all that time, why this mad scramble now?'

'That would be your first experience of the celebrated military ethos known as hurrying up and waiting. CSE?'

I nodded.

'Comedian?'

'Not exactly…'

I explained.

Charlie commented, 'Incongruous.' Then, tilting his head toward the mad scrambling, he said, 'My mum's a secretary. This business of getting the thing done sharpish, then standing by for however long, reminds her of the old-school way of training a typist to use the space bar. You were taught to always think of pressing the space bar when you'd typed the latest word, and not to think of pressing the space bar *before* typing the upcoming word – because you could never be sure if and when that next word might come.'

I got the impression that any time now Charlie might feel that he had done his duty in allowing me to raise his morale and would say his goodbyes.

I said, 'They're all diving in, grabbing wildly – yet it always turns out to be the right bag.'

'I would think that's something akin to the way a mother in a maternity ward would go straight to her uncustomised baby among many other uncustomised babies.'

From Basra airport to the actual base we took a recommissioned Home Counties school bus, complete with sandbags against blasts and gingham curtains at the windows. A number of squaddies came with us, to be dropped just past somewhere called the APOD.

Andy Askins said, 'This bus is a reconditioned pile of junk, right? Its bright orange colour has for some reason been retained, the chrome is fake, it's damp, there's sand everywhere – but the military has gone to the trouble of putting up these pretty gingham curtains. Let's join in nicely and draw them… and open them… draw them… and open them… draw…' He then led us in 'One Man Went to Mow'.

I looked out at sharp lights, barbed wire and anti-blast wall in all directions to our left; the black softness of the desert to the right; fires on the horizon.

'Burning the oil to stop the Americans getting it,' Ian explained.

Helicopters, armoured cars and what looked like a baby tank loomed and receded.

'One of ours,' Andy Askins would reassure us each time, breaking off from singing.

'Oops' – this in reaction to the baby tank – '*not* one of ours. Quick – duck!'

Smiles and eye rolling from the squaddies.

Who might be out there in the darkness? Were they plotting? My points of reference for military plotting were black-and-white films, in which everyone spoke with the upper-class accent that rendered the contemporary euphemism for homosexual – 'He is not a marrying man' – as 'He is naht a mee-air-ee-ing mee-ern.' There were always WRAFs in the films playing battleships with croupiers' sticks; and a mutt left without its master would have a scene looking mournfully at a pipe rack, hip flask and be posthumously awarded Order of the Garter.

But this, now, here, was real. Oh, and contemporary. Which I don't do. I sound like bad opera crossover, singing anything composed after 1925, and I must never dance ballet choreographed later than 1896, as my grand, Imperial style bruises its nuance.

No, here was a real, contemporary war zone – Iraq – and in it, me, tutu, Swan Queen tiara, on an open desert road, in a rickety little bus bolstered with sandbags.

What could those possibly do if we got shelled? The gingham curtains would offer more protection. (I might just duck down in my seat below the level of the glass, actually.) Did sandbags even stop 54a Crag Path, Aldeburgh, getting detritus in it when the sea came over the wall? No, they didn't. That's why the rats moved in in such numbers: food supply fecundity.

I want to get off this bus.

Is the base near enough to walk?

How can Tonks, Rhod and Gina sleep? Andy's giggling with Nicky. Spoons and Ian are talking football…

And what about the squaddies?

Oh, really – looking so unconcernedly out of the window we could be on the number 19 bus going through Highbury Barn?

As it turned out, the base *was* close enough to have walked. We dropped the squaddies off and reversed some 30 yards back down the road. An armed guard stepped out of a sentry box that would have been quite Horse Guards, except it wasn't an unscathed white tourist trap, but dung-coloured and bullet-holed. Our driver showed his pass and the guard saluted us through the barrier into a compound. Just inside, a squaddie flagged the bus down. At his feet was a cardboard box. Floodlighting picked out a fire-blackened car, a cluster of prefabs and some Portaloos. A low, hulking wall snaked all around, running parallel with a black plastic walkway. Again the bray and fuel smell coming from generators.

Off the bus I got a proper look at the squaddie. On *Victory* he had been in regimental dress, and my gaze went to his bare throat and forearms.

'You were right, Nicky,' I said. 'I'd recognise that scowl any-where.'

'Told you. He does quite a bit of CSE liaison because of his background in the arts.'

'Of all the bases in all the war zones in all the world…' said Stacks, as we shook hands. 'It's the man with the kryptonite lungs.'

'Really?' Nicky wondered.

'Decibel count off the scale. But I take it you're not out here to sing, but will be doing your Madame Galina? We've nicknamed the show *Four Comics and It*.'

'Clearly still overdosing on the Discovery Channel.'

'Help yourselves to the bag-rats in this box, peeps,' he said.

'Bag rations,' Ian clarified.

Chocolate, custard creams, an apple and a carton of orange juice.

Stacks stood midway to attention. 'Good evening and welcome, oh funny funsters. I'm Stacks, liaison officer at the APOD, Basra, for this – what I've been severely harassed by both your end and mine to call – *historic* artistic occasion. Over the wire of late the locals have been having a lot of weddings, so they're more involved in slow-dancing their nephews than in attacking us. We occasionally send up a warning shot or two to encourage them to cool it with the Demis Roussos. Wear your body armour around camp. When you leave it on a shelf over at *scoff*, it must take you no longer than two minutes, should it become necessary, to put it on. Scoff, by the way – food – is not a jokey reference to the chef Escoffier. If you hear the attack alarm, immediately get under hard cover and wait there till the guys have secured the area and you hear the all-clear. One bit of really bad news – we're in a dry camp.'

'No booze,' Ian put in.

Stacks gave him a brief, freezing glance.

'Your accommodation is on base and already fully built, rather than being a yomp into the desert and something you yourselves have to put up. Gents, you're right there.' He pointed to the nearest prefab, tucked away beneath an awning a sharp left from the entrance to the base. 'Ladies, I'll be taking you over when you want to turn in. Nobody else will be in your billets with you. At least not tonight. The ablutions are opposite, the gym left along over there, the scoff house over yonder. Talking of which: not too impressed by the bag-rats, are we? I'll drive you down the road for Pizza Hut or Subway.'

'Yeah, right,' I said. 'Is there a Dorothy Perkins?'

'Oh, ye of little faith.'

A short drive away were both Pizza Hut and Subway. They were housed in prefabs, but otherwise had the universal branded food, drink and hoardings. No Dorothy Perkins.

We bought food with US dollars, getting plastic tokens instead of coins in the change, and sat at picnic tables surrounded by storage containers.

'How weird to think that's the same moon.' As last seen through my bedsit window above The Lord Stanley. With a pang of homesickness, added to my panic, I thought of Mogatroyd on the gatepost and Bernard reading among the oil paintings.

Stacks said, 'Coming out to Iraq or Afghanistan is like being beamed down off the *Starship Enterprise*, and this time Scottie's well and truly fucked up the co-ordinates.'

The musty summer-holiday smell of the gents' billet prefab, *Male Holding Accommodation*, was overlaid with diesel. At the far end were metal lockers, most against the wall, but some freestanding; I suspected after a hunt for camel spiders. (I had my own hunt for camel spiders.) Bunk beds lined another wall, single cots opposite. Holes had been punched out of all the walls. Grey lino. No curtains or blinds at the windows.

Ian handed out bedding rolls and I felt my new-boy status being reinforced as I watched him quickly make base camp. He hung his clothes from a metal ridge in the wall, his towel over a chair, ranged his boots beneath his bed, his pillow, clock radio and phone charger on a chair beside it.

I responded by taking my spare tutu out of the Primark bag to use as a pillow.

Tonks was in the single bed next to mine, then Spoons. Opposite Spoons was Andy Askins; Rhod Gilbert was nearest the door. All were very quiet over their unpacking – markedly so. I thought back over Stacks's induction speech – had he ordered us to be quiet? Who might overhear? Couldn't remember.

How can the others sleep?
I so want to go home. Ten days of this otherness.
I feel like I'm a drawing that's been partially rubbed out.

Nobody can possibly like my act out here. They'll boo, they'll chuck stuff and the officers won't step in because that would flatten morale.

The musty smell is like when I first get to 54a Crag Path, Aldeburgh, for holidays. Open and click the bathroom door a few times, check that the books are still on the mantelpiece in the sitting room: Diary of a Provincial Lady, Know Your Knots *and* Coping with Catarrhal Deafness.

What was that noise?

I'm locked into that female persona again; thinking as her. I last remember doing this when I was renting the converted garage on the marshes and there were too many windows, not enough curtains, an overkill of moon. Come out of it, come out of it...

More noise just then.

Might it be the desert wind?

Or desert foxes going through the bins?

Fucking hell, it's ack ack ack ack. Ack. Ack. And... oh... that was more of a doof.

Awake now, are we, Mr and Mr Others in here?

'I Hear the Sound of Distant Drums'. Who sang that? Tex Withers stopped singing at the Ponderosa in Portsmouth when he saw the owner of the club come into the main room and shouted: 'Jesus fucking Christ, there's the little cow who had his coat off to me outside. I'd have knocked him to the ground.'

The ack ack ack and the doof didn't go on very long. Maybe whoever it was is a good shot and hits targets first time. Or maybe it was an insurgent gun salute for a new bride!

There was a gun salute when the Calais swordsman executed Anne Boleyn.

Actually, did they have guns back then?

I'll ask Stacks. I wonder where he is? Does he have his own room or share? Can he sleep out here? I can imagine he has one of those little white alarm clocks, from Argos.

If the noise just now were a gun salute, explain the rogue doof?

Hear that shuffling noise now? Sounds like something crawling on eight hairy, straw-like legs.

Is eczema hereditary?

Jim Reeves sang 'Distant Drums'.

Chapter Seven

I was awake just after nine. The winter light didn't make sense with the British summer temperature.

'Cool dressing gown there,' Tonks whispered, putting aside the book he was reading.

'Primark. The horizontal stripes are slimming. All about the morale-raising.'

I asked him what he thought the audiences would be like out here in Iraq.

'Up for it,' he replied. 'There's so little else going on out here by way of distraction.'

'But they'll normally have seen stand-up – not anything remotely like my act.'

He nodded, exhaling slowly. 'Mate, Nicky would hardly have brought you out here on purpose to die on your arse. Know your targets, bit like I'll be doing in my note-taking: that officer they all dislike; the Company joker; the flash bastard. And get in among them.'

I was grateful to him, though hardly reassured.

Getting my toiletries out of my case, I found that, in my state of fear back in St Pancras, I had packed a plant sprayer, tin foil, a fork and a head of garlic.

'Take your body armour, Iestyn,' Ian reminded me as I crept to the door on my way to the ablutions.

Sighing, I crept back to my bed and lumbered myself with metal helmet and body armour. Right, this needed thinking about: how to get me, the body armour, my wash kit and my towel across to the ablutions. I put the body armour on over my dressing gown, draped the towel over my arm and carried my helmet upturned by its chin straps, filled with my Lush smellies.

I said good morning on my way to an older-looking man – no wings... no swords... so army... crown... two diamonds... greatly important in army. He had accessorised his uniform with a neck-erchief, a woggle and green wellingtons. Clearly too skittish for the stage. Frowning briefly at my upturned helmet, he returned my greeting and disappeared behind some prefabs.

The ablutions were like any chrome-and-grey shower block seen in the UK, from Swansea caravan parks through Bestival to the Blackpool Pleasure Beach performers' digs.

There were laminated signs:

Thirty seconds get wet, switch off shower, lather up,
thirty seconds rinse off. Or we'll all be having to make
do with bottled water again, won't we?

I obeyed the instructions, idly wondering if there might be stric-tures on how long I must take towelling myself dry.

Back at the accommodation, I dressed in shorts and T-shirt and was shouldering my body armour to go out and explore when Ian asked us all to stow our sleeping bags. 'First show isaway at Camp Smitty, and we may – but hopefully not – be forced to stay there overnight, for whatever reason.'

Rhod asked, 'What might one of the reasons be, Ian?'

'Soft option or hard option?'

'For openers, let's go with soft.'

'Lack of transport.'

'Hard?'

'An incident.'

'By which I take it you don't mean overkill heckling?'

The mention of the show and then heckling nearly made me cry out.

'It's like having a baby in reverse, isn't it?' Spoons said, strug-gling with his sleeping roll. 'A full-size, adult sleeping bag has to be spooled back in on itself to end up being just slightly bigger than a Peak Freans fig roll.'

Mine took me a good seventeen 'fuck sakes'. I looped it to my tutu bag and went outside. Keeping a look out for creeping things and insurgency attack I stuck close to the anti-blast wall. The colour of meringue, made up of separate pods, the wall came to chest height, was about a metre and a half thick and was filled with concrete and sand.

'Are you going to try it in your mouth next?'

I stopped sniffing the chicken wire that covered the top and sides of each pod. Stacks was sitting at a table beneath a steel awning slung over aluminium props. Behind him, beyond the wire, mountains rose the colour of faded ink.

'Tea for the artiste?' he asked, indicating a tray laid with polystyrene cups, silver teapot, caddy and highly ornate tea strainer. 'Just brewed.'

I went and sat opposite him on a folding chair, stuffing my body armour and helmet underneath.

He said, 'That helmet, mate, is for your protection and not for you to carry your wash stuff over to the ablutions in.'

'Sorry, sir,' I said. 'But I did abide by the sign on the wall saying thirty seconds get wet, water off, lather up, thirty seconds water on to rinse; and I stood there going, "A thousand and one, a thousand and two, a thousand and three…" and got a mouth full of skanky water.'

'Sea shower regulations: you're a moral beacon.' He handed me some tea.

I asked, 'At some point would it be all right for me to make a bucket of tea with milk?'

'Wouldn't a few Red Bulls do you?'

'Need to dye white ballet tights.' As flesh-coloured ballet tights are much more expensive than white, I buy white ones and dye them in tea. 'I didn't have time to get teabags from the Co-op. Luckily, I'm doing Nikiya out here, not nasty, jilted Gamzatti. For her, I have to dye my whole tutu. I use three bags. One for each "tu" and one for the pot. Oh, and Stacks – I find my leg muscles look more defined in stage lighting if I use Darjeeling.'

His left eyebrow was virtually under his green beret. 'If you get any stage lights. The CSE technical equipment got bumped off the flight from Brize. It's going to be a ghetto-blaster-and-torches job.'

Sipping my tea, I scanned the ground. He followed my gaze. 'Camel spiders,' I explained.

'They'll be asleep in this weather. Quite a snuggly breed of creature when you get to know them. How did you sleep, first night out in theatre? Did you hear the shelling? Enemy attacking the railway station.'

'Might they not need to go somewhere?'

'Occupying forces' supply trains, not the oasis express. Confused? You will be.'

He added that while he was sure CSE did all they could to prepare us for a trip out to theatre – stuff to pack, security dos and don'ts, and so on – what I really needed was the bootneck 'How to Prepare for Deployment'.

'Bootneck?' I wondered.

'Royal Marine. I'll run you off a copy.'

Shelling started somewhere over the wire. 'Woah!' I hauled myself out of the chair. 'Woah!' I was squirming so much as I put on my body armour I nearly fell onto the tea table.

'At ease,' Stacks said. He gestured toward the wire. 'Obviously there are only so many times you can say how pretty the bride looks, moan about how much the reception's costing you, have sex with the bridesmaids in cleaning cupboards – they're just making a bit of noise wending their way home with a balloon, party bag, cake in a napkin.'

'But shouldn't we—?'

'No. Rule of thumb is, if *I* (service personnel) do anything, then you know that *you* (civilian) have to do something.'

There was a particularly big explosion. I shut my eyes and held my breath.

'Chill. We've had two direct hits in the last fourteen or so launches. And they were only direct hits insofar as they got over the wire and onto the actual base. They were nowhere near anyone or anything of importance. The insurgents have the rockets, but not the launchers, which leaves them improvising. Recent intelligence reports them launching a rocket off a bit of old bedstead.

It's out on the roads where the danger is. We'll only take you that way if we really have to, and that'll be in an armed convoy. Otherwise you'll go by helicopter. You'll also have another armed guard other than me; someone extra-huge, ripped and mean. Michelle. Driving us to the airheads to fly to Smitty later. Oh, now… think on…' He was eyeballing me. (I came to recognise two distinct ways that Stacks had of eyeballing me. The first was like a roustabout watching drunk girls get into his Waltzer car. The second always reminded me of what my farmer mate Will once said, capping a familiar adage: dogs think humans are wonderful because they feed them, cats think humans are a load of shit – but a black pot-bellied pig will always look you right in the eye.) 'Think on…' He was giving me the pig look. 'I've heard—'

'Oh, fuck!' I was up out of my seat again at more battle noise from over the wire.

'Chill,' Stacks said. 'I'm sitting still, aren't I? They're just shelling the railway station again. Must have missed Tariq the Tank Engine first go around. Now…' More of the pig look. 'I've heard you get people up out of the audience to join in with your act. Leave me out of that or there'll be consequences.' I saw that he was deadly serious. 'Understood?'

I nodded.

Back in the accommodation an hour or so later, Andy Askins was making us watch his recreation of the one-man luge. 'Just need my helmet…'

He put it on and, with his arms rigid at his side, feet turned in, made a juddering movement that coursed through his whole body, tilting his head to right and left to show changes of direction down the course, imitating perfectly the effect of the g-force hitting his face.

There was a knock on the door. A ripped and mean-looking blonde stood on the threshold. There was a waft of expensive perfume, her hair was in a French pleat, her voice silk-scarf Highlands.

'Guys, I'm Michelle, here just now to take you to lunch scoff. All of you got your body armour on?'

'Good God,' said Ian, checking us all over as we stepped outside. 'They're all wearing it. Michelle – put it in your report later. It's a moment in history to rank alongside a tree-hopper getting trapped in amber during the Cretaceous period.'

Spoons was crossing the compound from the direction of Stacks's awning.

'What's the latest?' Nicky asked him.

'Equipment was bumped off the plane at Brize. It'll be out here when it's out here. Meanwhile, there are rumours of a Dutch priest having his very own halogen lamp.'

The walls of the dining hall were whitewashed, the floor concrete, lit by energy-saving strip bulbs. Michelle pointed us to some wooden shelves. 'Store your body armour here, guys,' she said. 'And please make a careful note of exactly where yours is. Next, wash your hands, dry them and treat them with the disinfectant gel. *Then* collect your tray, plate, cutlery and so forth.'

I passed her to put my body armour on a shelf. 'Sorry if I sound patronising,' she said.

'Not at all. I've never done this before; and I like not having to think for myself.'

'Lots of different shades of camouflage,' Gina said.

Ranging from the Dutch being lightest, through the Brits to the Americans with the darkest uniforms.

'The Americans are wearing grey,' Rhod said. 'What's that about?'

Michelle said, 'Going into villages and seeking out suicide bombers.'

On the lunch menu – 'As I survey the wondrous scoff,' Andy sang – were chicken chasseur, lamb korma, beef stroganoff and vegetarian moussaka. Rhod helped himself to all four.

'While I'm out here I'm going to eat like a total bastard.'

Joining us for crème brûlée, Stacks gave me the Marines' photocopied 'How to Prepare for Deployment':

1. Invite one hundred and eighty-five people to stay. They must all have bizarre hygiene habits. You must all exchange underwear.

2. Leave a lawnmower fuelled by Vaseline running constantly in your sitting room.

3. Sprinkle fish-tank gravel through your flat; put it in your bed, in your pants, on your soap, in your Nutella.

4. Shoot holes in your walls from both inside and out.

5. Sleep on a camp bed in the garage. Replace the garage door with tarpaulin. Each time you drop off, one of the people staying should time six minutes, pull the tarpaulin aside and shine a torch in your eyes. 'Sorry, wrong tent!'

6. Move the shower head down to spray at your belly button. Keep four inches of soapy cold water in the shower tray. Shower in pitch darkness. Wear flip flops. Only one, actually. The left one.

7. Stop cleaning the toilet approximately four years before you're due for deployment. Resist all notions of aiming. Only when pissing, obviously. You're not a complete animal. Remove all toilet paper other than two sheets at the end of the roll. Actually, remove it altogether.

8. Come again – arrange to use a neighbour's toilet. A neighbour who lives at least two tram changes away. Go with your own two sheets of toilet paper, in your dressing gown and that one left flip flop. Oh, silly me, we haven't got the two sheets of toilet paper anymore, have we?

9. Let off 50 Thunder King fireworks simultaneously

outside at three in the morning. When startled neighbours appear, tell them all is well, you are just registering mortars. Tell them plastic will make an acceptable substitute for their blown-in windows. Order them to dig an emergency survival pit with overhead cover in their garden. Inspect it and find that it's not to spec – the 4x4s aren't precisely eight inches apart, or some similar bollocks – and make them rebuild it. Constantly.

10. Put grobags on the floor of your car to withstand mine blasts. Stop at each flyover, alleyway or hedge to make an inspection for remotely detonated explosives. Tell anyone that may stop to ask what the hell you're doing that you're RSPB and there's been reports of a goshawk running amok.

11. Cut your own hair by feel alone.

12. Once a month, take every major appliance in your house apart and immediately put it back together again.

13. Put a pile of books against the threshold of your front door so that you hit your head every time you pass through it. Dig down a few inches at the threshold to the back door so you trip on that each time. Alternate the books and the pit once every two to three weeks.

14. Eat an M&M every Sunday and convince yourself it will immunise you against malaria.

15. Announce to the 185 people staying with you that there is post for them. They must report to you individually as you stand outside your open garage door after evening scoff. When it's finally their turn, they must sign in triplicate before you say, 'Sorry, it's for the other Smith.'

16. Roll your regimental dress in a ball. Leave it in the corner of the garage where the cat pisses to percolate for a fortnight. Wear to official military functions.

17. Go to the worst crime-infested place in Manchester heavily armed, wearing body armour and a Kevlar helmet. Set up shop in a tent in a car park. Tell the locals that you are there to help them.

Chapter Eight

Stacks called us to order on the bus. 'Body armour, bed roll, spare knickers, wet wipes, condoms, asthma inhalers, flask of warm milk, vitamin pills, pair of bed socks, single wank-sock, PMT tablets, reading material – in short, whatever you might need for an overnight stay away from this beautifully administered camp in case we get stuck at Smitty. We'll be going from here to the airheads, transferring onto a helicopter. The helicopter may be running late, as I hear we have a Brigadier in the vicinity just now and he mistakenly thinks that he has a greater need for it.' Readjusting his rifle like an archer his bow, he sat in the front passenger seat. 'If you would, please, Michelle.'

Focused, scanning his surroundings, he looked massive, adept and self-possessed.

Behind us were the white prefabs of the NAAFI stores. A helicopter hung overhead. Vehicles passed and the fires burnt. Tonks and Andy were swapping stories of tough squaddie audiences. Listening, I imagined that this must be what it was like for new prisoners on a bus with old lags.

'Do you remember that poor guy who was opening in Basra?' Andy said. 'Lost his thread and said: "Just give me a minute, lads." The Marines were straight in with the countdown: "Sixty... fifty-nine... fifty-eight..."'

Do you remember Archie? He was in solitary for sixteen years. Came out convinced he was Mary Queen of Scots.

Tonks said, 'He was being a smart arse with the Paras in the Falklands and they canned him off. Then their game after that for the rest of the tour was to can him off before he'd got out so much as: "Good evening, great to be out here with you."'

Poor Bernard – sent to the psych wing for what he saw in the Rorschach Ink Blot.

Tonks again: 'He should never have let the Guards talk him

into bodysurfing. His own fault that by the third row he was all but minus his bollocks.'

His money wasn't transferred when they moved him to another nick. Couldn't get smokes, or extras from the canteen. He was crying, emailing his MP, pelting the screws with anything and everything he could shit in his hand.

We stopped briefly while Michelle and Stacks spoke to the driver of an armoured jeep going in the opposite direction. I couldn't catch what was being said.

A few feet from the road were three camels.

'Which means the Wise Men are having a piss behind that clump of rocks,' said Rhod.

I wound down a window to offer the camels a custard cream.

They weren't keen.

'Where's this place?' I asked Stacks.

'Airheads.'

'Oh.'

'Where you landed last night.'

'Looks totally unfamiliar.'

'Last night was the arrivals lounge.' He made a flourish. 'Welcome to departures, sir.'

A passenger jet, a spindly black helicopter and an aeroplane like a basking shark were parked on the near side of the runway.

'Peeps, forty-five minutes here to kill,' Stacks said. 'There's tea over in the workshop right; maybe even a few biscuits.'

Lieutenant Mitchell took our tea and coffee orders. He had curls like fried mince and his eyelids were too big for him. He spoke almost in a whisper, turning to face each person at precise right angles as he asked if they wanted tea or coffee, and then milk and sugar? Ian asked for tea with a cow and a couple of Julies.

Lieutenant Mitchell asked again if Ian wanted milk and sugar, sir?

'Cow and a couple of Julies, please.'

'Sir, milk and sugar?'

'Cow and a couple of Julies, thanks.'

'Sir...'

They went back and forth like this till Stacks threatened violence.

Aside from the gigantic plasma-screen TV, the holding bay might have been a defunct corner of IKEA. Stacks, watching with Rhod and Tonks, smiled archly at me. 'Footie, princess?'

'No, thank you. But remember, children, don't get anxious – there's really no such thing as the offside rule.'

In the opposite corner a woman was sitting drinking coffee out of a flask. She was plump with knotty black hair swirled under her uniform cap. I asked if I could join her.

She nodded. 'I would like that.'

She was US Army Captain Miriam Bennington. I briefly thought of asking her outright to tell me things would be fine; she must try as hard as she could to make it sound convincing and I would try to make myself believe her. She said that her 22 years' service had finished the previous May and she had signed up for extended time. 'To train the Iraqi army. Which is easier said than done, believe me!' Each day for the first two weeks of her lectures, one or other of her students had reported Miriam for speaking to men before she had been spoken to. 'Finally, *finally*, during my most recent class, not only did none of them leave to snitch on me, but one of them asked me a question. An actual question, imagine that. True, he asked if I was married and did my husband permit all my free behaviour...'

There was a metallic wheeze as the door opened behind me.

'Photo opportunity, Iestyn,' Nicky called. 'Let's make the most of the delay; come and put your tutu on.'

I apologised to Miriam and went outside.

Behind the wall, I dressed in my full stage rig, keeping an eye out for anything that might land when I was knickerless. Ian snapped me on the runway with a backdrop of an Apache helicopter and some oil-wasting fires, being chased onto a passenger jet by Andy, Tonks, Rhod and Gina and performing *pas de chats* in and out of the Portaloo, designated 'For Diarrhoea and Vomiting Quarantine Only'.

When Stacks got word that the helicopter was due in any time now I dodged back behind the wall. Bending to untie my shoe ribbons, I looked for the approaching helicopter. It was a way off yet. I undid my right ribbon and, as the helicopter's drone changed to distinguishable *thwocks*, reached down for the left. I couldn't free the knot.

'Come on, come on,' I muttered, feeling air displaced by the helicopter blades rushing over me. When the knot finally gave, I slipped the shoe off, pulled my tutu over my head and made a grab at my knickers. The helicopter landed.

'Naomi Campbell over there – we're off,' Stacks shouted.

I thought I would be safe to pull my knickers down beneath my T-shirt.

There was an unhelpful gust from the taxiing helicopter.

I hoped that just then the Brigadier wasn't looking out of the VIP porthole.

Clapping his hands, Stacks began. 'Right, peeps, finally. In a short while—' He fell silent as the Brigadier with entourage came this side of the wall. The only Brigadier I'd ever seen before was an operagoer at the Royal Opera House, and he had been neatly made and giggly. This present Brigadier was towering and awesome. He wore a beret, medals and a sneer, and spoke to me in regal Home Counties. 'A most interesting welcoming committee.'

I bowed to him. There were not-quite-stifled guffaws around me. 'No,' I said to the Brigadier, 'I wasn't being sarcastic bowing. It's just that… that…'

Expectancy all round. I looked up at the Brigadier. 'That…'

Still more expectancy.

'… well, I've only seen one, small Brigadier before – and you're *huge*.'

'Gentlemen,' he said, and his escort surrounded him like so many pilot fish at a whale shark's gills.

Stacks said, 'I can only imagine the complaint that'll go into the APOD office from that mardy fuck. Now, please, you'll walk in single file out across the airfield to the back of the helicopter, then up the ramp, again in single file. Don't look at the propeller. It has a mesmerising effect like a flute on a snake. People have been known to take a running jump into it.'

He had to be joshing, though his look was guileless.

The sun was directly on us. The noise from the helicopter was enervating. I leant into the buffeting, displaced airstream. Sudden heat and a stink of petrol hit as I teetered up the ramp at the back. Light on board was through portholes, seats faced inward set into walls encrusted with dials. There was space for baggage in the centre. I kept my tutu bag safe over my wrist. At a window three quarters of the way down on each side a gun was mounted. One of the flight crew, a Prince William clone, directed us to seats. He winked at me and held up a camera. Cupping my hand over it I looked at the photo displayed. It was of me apparently mooning the Brigadier. I asked him not to put it up on Facebook. (He has.)

A counterpart to Prince William was helping Spoons and Stacks tie down a metal case. Prince William gave Tonks a paper bag and indicated that he should pass it round; Tonks picked two yellow boxes out of the bag before handing it on to Rhod.

'Oh, earplugs,' I said. 'Not a sick bag for sharing.'

Final checks and then, wasp-like, the helicopter rose into the air and thrust forward. Prince William and counterpart sat behind the guns, peering past them at the ground. Stacks was looking about him as though he wanted to be doing something. Through a porthole I watched the airfield give way to desert road, a straggling white stone bungalow, burnt-out cars and a caravan of camels.

After half an hour or so Prince William went along the two lines of seats and made us all show him that we were belted in. We flew over clumps of date palms, then parallel to a ravine with a single row of square two-storey houses along its floor, windows facing us.

Amid panicked screams the helicopter dropped straight at the ground.

'Shitting heck, did we need that bit of trick flying?' Spoons was asking.

We had landed safely at Camp Smitty and were mustering around Stacks at the edge of the runway.

'Didn't you see the air guy give me his camera?' Gina wondered. 'Asked me to take a photo of him lying on the ceiling when the helicopter went into negative gravity.'

'Just frightening civilians,' said Stacks. 'Though the Welsh opera singer with the rack did have a properly close shave in a helicopter.' If Katherine Jenkins's danger had been real, and mine a sham, what chance had I of eclipsing her and becoming Forces' Sweetheart? 'They should discipline the Crab twats. Last time I flew home from Afghanistan, the pilot got a serious smacked wrist for putting out a message: "And this is one for the ladies on board. Now that we're back in Blighty, your attractiveness rating will adjust itself back down in accordance with reality."' Watching the helicopter trundling along, he added, 'You may get a flares show, if they have some onboard past the safe-use date.'

As the helicopter passed overhead, sulphurous blues and greens crackled and fizzed to earth.

A squaddie emerged from the smoke. Behind him were white, flat-roofed hangars that, peeling, scuffed and lit by winter sun, had a look of off-season Torquay. He had a sphinx-wide face, blond curls and wore a mint-green T-shirt, brown short-shorts and flopping, grey ankle wellies.

'Typical fucking Para,' Stacks commented out of the corner of his mouth that was nearest me. 'Oh, but from the look on your face I see he's chalked up at least a score of one.'

'He's *stunning*,' I gasped, picturing the moment the Swan

Queen gently cups the Prince's face, before he folds her wings and leans her on his hip in total surrender. 'And I've got just the right tiara!'

'Pardon me?' said the Para. He stopped walking; his wellies lurched.

'Nothing. Sorry.'

'Sirs and ma'am, proud to welcome you to Camp Smitty today, on behalf of the awesome Company that is 2 Para. I'm Captain Sam Ashton – for obvious reasons known as "Prettiest Boy". If you'd please like to make your way with me.'

Andy asked Stacks, 'Why did you call the helicopter guys "Crab twats"?'

Sam cut in. 'The RAF are known as Crab Airways because only them out of the three armed services are allowed to step sideways as many times as they like during drill. The rest of us are only allowed three steps. If the mood takes them, RAF personnel can march sideways over the whole parade ground. And so often do. And as the big old Merlin engine on the front of a Spitfire was too big to see past straight on, they had to be taxied sideways with the pilot leaning out of the cockpit to check where he was going. So taking all with all: the amount of sideways movement – Crabs.'

Stacks said that most of what Sam had just told us was bollocks. 'The Navy gave the RAF the nickname Crabs. RAF uniforms were the same shade of blue as the ointment that sailors put on the crabs inevitably caught during shore leave. The ointment came to be known as Crab Fat, so the RAF came to be called Crab Fats, shortened over time to Crabs.'

Sam actually said 'Pah!', then added that the Navy were known as Bum Boys or Fish Heads; the army as Pongoes, from 'Where the army goes, the pong goes'. Royal Marines were Bootnecks or The Green Death. Tank Division: Tankies, Canned Veg or GRUNTS (Government Reject Unfit for Normal Training).

'Security check,' Sam announced, gesturing through a doorway at two military policemen. One was tall, blond and sloping, the other bald and hugely muscled. There was a strong smell of diesel about him.

'ID.'

Nicky Ness, Ian and everyone else showed their driver's licences. I said, 'I haven't got a driving licence. I can't drive. I gave up lessons. I had this really horrible instructor with a tramp's beard. I was simply trying to make the information he was giving me chime with myself by pointing out that the car revving to biting point went from the keynote up a perfect fourth, like at the beginning of "Bel Raggio Lusinghier", sung by Semiramide, Queen of Babylon. He very snidely asked me not to weird him out saying stuff like that as I was frightening him quite enough with my lack of clutch control. Me frightening *him*? What about how slippery his shoes had been on the dual controls? Looking like they'd been made out of badly moulded liquorice and burnt spaghetti.'

No question that right now I was being the CSE tour 'What the f… ?' factor. The sloping policeman asked, 'Passport?'

'I've left my passport back at Basra under my spare tutu. I've been using it as a pillow. Oh, talking of tutus: look, I'm on that CSE poster behind you wearing one.' And here it was in the flesh, as it were, pulled out of its Primark bag. 'Otherwise, I'll have to show you my Camden library card. But please can you not stop me doing the gig, or I'd be out here in Iraq irrelevantly.'

There was grey industrial carpet in the CSE Green Room; as yet no holes punched out of the walls. A trestle table was laid with a white paper cloth, plates and napkins. Nicky had pre-ordered fruit, crisps and Minstrels.

'Locust storm or what?' Sam commented, watching us rush the trestle table.

Nicky said, 'Running order. Tonks compère, Rhod on first, then Andy, then, after the interval, Gina and Madame Galina.'

She asked Sam who we would have out front for the show.

'Us and the Australian Army.'

'2Para and the Aussie army for a new-format gig,' said Nicky.

I caught her eye and she looked immediately away. 'Eye of the storm.'

Sam said, 'Hoping our lad up for a bravery medal will be here for you to meet later. We had a bit of a hit last week. Enemy surprised about twenty of us on foot out in the open. Hitting us with small arms and grenades from everywhere and anywhere. We must have been outnumbered two to one. Road surface so potholed you had to look down at where you were putting your feet the whole time, so getting a firing rhythm going was virtually impossible. I thanked God, Allah and *fuck for that* when I saw the Land Rover. Driven into the middle of the fire by a certain Sergeant James Newell. Put that name on a tankard to hang in your local. Jimbo jumped out of the Land Rover and returned fire, picked up four of us at a time, drove to this operations centre we'd previously rigged up – we had some cover at least there – then went back for the next four, and again, till we were all in the centre. Jimbo's up for showing repeated and premeditated disregard for personal safety honours. Said he'd never experienced anything like that in all his past shouts out here, Ghanners and Northern Ireland.'

I looked at Stacks, expecting some heckling remark. He was nodding slowly, watching Sam.

Sam said, 'Right, let's head to the venue.'

Stacks stopped me at the door. 'Body armour?'

'On the table next to the Pringles.'

'Ah, talking of which…'

He walked with me to the bowl of Minstrels and took a handful. Stowing them in a hanky, he put them in his pocket. 'For later.' Then he helped himself to another one and tried to peel it.

'Why are you doing that?' I asked, picking up my body armour.

'I like the chocolate part, but the shell does the same to my teeth as fingernails down a board. Shit the fucking thing – nails are what I could do with, actually.'

'Pass it here,' I said.

The venue was white colonial, 50 yards down from the Green Room. There were wooden benches in 20 or so rows, armchairs at right angles to the front row, a raised stage covered in damask patterned carpet.

Spoons was sitting at the technician's station just on the other side of a particularly frowzy green-and-mauve armchair. 'Please bear with me on the sound and lighting front tonight.'

He had brought to the gig the Dutch priest's halogen lamp and a CD player from an officers' mess. I imagined the mawkish music normally played on it to facilitate the clubbable-crony crying: Mahler symphonies, 'Jerusalem', 'Feed the Birds'.

Though the show wasn't due to start for another hour, a squaddie had already taken a seat in the front row. He was massive, number-two-cropped with an urchin's face, which would read easily right to the back of the venue.

'Iestyn,' I said, shaking hands, already looking forward to him lifting me.

'Sobs.'

'Do you cry a lot? Are you an officer?'

'Corporal. Sobs because of the stories I tell to get out of building deployment. Offices for generals to sit around in with their feet up having their tea and biscuits? No, cheers. I joined the Aussie army to fight the fuckers on the other side of the wire.'

'You're not from Australia,' I said.

'Derby.'

'Then why are you in the Aussie army?'

'The beach landings are more decorative.'

Tonks came and sat down, notebook in hand. 'Who's being a bit of a twat this tour?' he asked Sobs.

'Pick on our Major with the rubber-gloves fetish. He'll clean the ablutions himself just so's he can wear them. With the chamois shorts from Switzerland. And a hard-on.'

Fighting back panic in the Green Room I checked tights, pants and pink ballet shoes for scorpions and/or camel spiders and applied slap using my spare backing track CD for a mirror. Stacks pushed the door open as I was getting my diaphragm up and running with a bit of *Under Milk Wood*.

'Shitting Nora, that get-up is beyond the pale. No, come again, they're going to have to move the pale a fuck of a lot further away.' When he'd last seen me perform I was in black tie. I picked up my onstage shroud to cover my cleavage. 'Making sure you're not running late, away or amok,' he said.

Was I imagining it, or did he have his rifle slung now at a more workaday angle?

'Just going through my rituals,' I said, setting off for a cartoonish jog on the spot.

'Nicky says you might have a Para colonel to dance with. Reckons pretty-boy Sam and the major who likes the rubber gloves might be too fair game for everyone.' I nodded. 'How do you choose your victims back home?'

I quoted some of my Galina shtick. 'In Mother Russia, dance for Orekhovskaya gang: is always best man at Orthodox wedding. Is always godfather at Orthodox christening. Is always man with golden Kalashnikov at Orthodox kneecapping.' I dropped the accent. 'I tend to shy away from set-ups and go into the crowd with my sixth-sense radar. I am the son of a stage psychic, after all. The Gypsy Eirwen. Gave a legendary reading in Hemel Hempstead: "I've got Charlie coming through for this woman in the side balcony. Am I right? Now, love, Charlie says he's your father. Am I right? Says he didn't die of natural causes: ask your murdering bitch of a mother. Am I right?" Obviously I go with a set-up when it's the stag, the company CEO at the Christmas corporate, the highest grace rating clergyman at the Dean of Bocking's Flower Festival. But in the past I've had the person who's been set up leave the building, or be unable to use his hands because he's in fancy dress as a penis, or try and force his asthma inhaler on me.'

'Why the asthma inhaler?'

'Nikiya, my character, needs the kiss of life after a snake bite.'

'She should mix it with more blackcurrant. You wouldn't kneecap someone with a Kalashnikov, either: too big. You'd use a Tokarev pistol.'

'Another nugget from the Discovery Channel?'

'Just remember what I told *you* about me being out of bounds.'

He'd be wrong anyway onstage: always needing to have the last fucking word.

I was outside doing ballet barre, holding on to the anti-blast wall. Beyond it, squaddies were playing football. One of the players caught sight of me, did a double take, and gestured around at his teammates to look. Grinning, they waved, but made shushing signs before I could call out a greeting and pointed to where some local workers in blue overalls were at prayer.

I wondered how they came to be employed on the base. And if working for NATO was thought of as betrayal. I was still warming up when they finished their prayers. They stood up and watched me. Their manner wasn't quite friendly, but neither was it reproachful or outraged.broth

I remembered the last time I had prayed – really prayed – before a show. At the Leeds Festival. My Friday set had been horrendous, and I went to York first thing Saturday knowing I was going to need something with at least minster status.

I was doing the UK Play Comedy Tent, packed with mainly 17-year-old boys, just broken up from school and munted on MDMA. Backstage, I had bumped into Jason Baron, one of the Baron Brothers, a musical-comedy trio.

'Not quite Klub Kabaret this gig,' Jason had said. 'Strictly TTMAR...'

'TTMAR?'

'Take the Money and Run. Get them to turn your mike and your backing track up full blast, so you don't have to hear the crowd.'

I was the opening act. Far from being at full blast, my backing track didn't come on at all. The 17-year-olds looked at me in the silence. I looked at them. A curly-haired, shirtless lad with a build like a US college wrestler stood up and led the chanting: 'Put your tutu on your head, put your tutu on your head. You fat bastard, you fat bastard, put your tutu on your head.'

I fitted what I could of my act proper around the ensuing ten-minute potty-mouth slanging match. At one point, security pulled out a group of ten or so lads from the middle of the tent. They hadn't actually been heckling, but they were in my eye-line. I told one of them not to bother trying to pull the girl lying next to him: I had seen inside his sleeping bag and it wasn't nice. They were on their way to the stage to rout me when security got to them.

I came offstage and went into shock.

'Why have you made me come here and do this?' I blurted to Jill, the event promoter. She had such expensive hair and status-defining accessories, the velour tracksuit the colour of custard had to be a comfort choice.

She said, 'If you found it that traumatic, fine – you can go home now and I'll still pay you. You've just been taken out of your comfort zone of Klub Kabaret, Regency Rooms, Cobden Club gigs. Everyone's there to watch you. This lot are here to test you.'

A girl in a tie-dyed T-shirt and paisley sarong flapped out of the Comedy Tent.

'Please, you're going on again?' she shouted to me.

'The boys hated me!'

'No, you started it going back and forth, and they were on it. If they had hated you, you'd know. If you go back on...'

'... I am going back on...'

'Those boys near the front – the bruiser one that started the chanting. Look by their feet.'

'What for?'

She said the three little words you never want to hear: 'Bottles of piss.'

I made myself go back on. The slanging match kicked off again. I peered down at bruiser-boy's feet. He did indeed have bottles lined up. Which he didn't actually throw at me. But, still, in

York Minster I prayed that nothing like that Friday gig would happen Saturday.

Or ever again, for that matter. Most urgently to date, just now, in Iraq.

Doing *rondes de jambes en l'air*, holding a NATO anti-blast wall, I prayed.

A man of towering height emerged from behind the Green-Room prefab.

'You look important,' I called out.

Appearing slightly reluctant, he changed course mid-lope. 'Rupert Curtis.'

'Iestyn Edwards, Madame Galina, er... crown... minus any possible wings... two stars... er... Colonel.'

He nodded, smiling beatifically. 'You'll have a couple of us in the show today. Melton, the 2 Para CO. And poss... oh, hello.' He was looking out across the five-a-side pitch to where five armoured cars were pulling up. 'Not to worry, guards are onto it.'

The guards were skirting the pitch at a jog. About 20 or so squaddies got out of the cars. They chatted briefly to the two guards, who then pointed to the venue.

'Royal Marines,' said Colonel Curtis. 'In quite some numbers, too. Their base is a way away, so they're not strictly meant to be here.'

I said, 'Please excuse me while I goose-step. And do you know my new friend the First Sea Lord?'

'Sir Alan's a good friend of mine.'

'If anything kicks off in there, anti-my-act sort of thing, you'll pull rank? As Nicky – Nicky Ness – puts it, the squaddies have a pack mentality. If they go with it, they'll go with it as one. If they don't, they'll turn as one. And they're known to be really hard, aren't they, Paras?'

'That is rather the point of them. Er, by the way, are you within two minutes of your body armour? I can't see it anywhere.'

Sighing, I hurtled back in the direction of the Green Room.

Chapter Nine

I lifted my body armour off the Minstrels table.

'But... but...'

The helmet was too small to wear over my Swan Queen tiara. (Clipping the tiara to the side of the helmet as before would now be *hors de question* because I wouldn't be going onstage *wearing* the helmet. Dame Margot Fonteyn would never have done such a thing – not even when she danced in London at the height of the Blitz.)

'And... and...'

When I carried the body armour over my arm, it hung down and flattened my tutu skirt.

'I... I...'

Would simply have to wear the body armour and carry the helmet in a suitably balletic manner.

I peeked through a window at Gina onstage. The venue was packed, rapt silence alternating with laughter. Gina signed off. Tonks acknowledged how brilliant she had just been – there was a bay of agreement – and announced that now we had some culture. I turned from the window to look at the wire behind me. I could climb it and take my chances with the insurgents.

'We're pushing the envelope here,' Tonks was saying. 'We've got some ballet. From a true prima ballerina. Fresh from a series for Channel 4, a private performance for Her Majesty and the Olivier Award-winning *C'est Barbican*: please give it up for Madame Galina, Ballet Star Galactica!'

The wire or the Tchaikovsky, the wire or the Tchaikovsky, the...

I was opening with the 'Entrance of Princess Aurora' and, as always, reminded myself of the correction Stella Beddard, my ballet teacher, had once given me: 'Princess Aurora needs to be much more delicate as you run on down the staircase. She is the embodiment of her Fairy Godmothers' gifts: grace, ease of articulation, wealth and temperament. You must suggest a fairy-tale princess seeming to materialise in the colonnade to dance sweetly for the guests at her coming-of-age celebrations. Not Godzilla boosting itself out of the Thames to set about County Hall.'

One and two and three and – I pulled open the door and appeared trippingly on stage. Heel-toe/heel-toe/heel-toe/heel-toe down an imaginary staircase in the approved non-Godzilla-like manner. The squaddies stared at me. I glanced at Nicky. She winked. Later she would write in her tour report: 'Show One. A stunning run of stand-up, there's no denying the well-tested talent, but then, the cross-dressing ballerina. The "what-the-f**k?" incredulity. A blinding flash of career before my eyes.'

The music for my dance was only a matter of seconds away and I took the run-up for my first *pas de chat*.

I was still wearing my body armour and carrying my helmet.

'Prettiest Boy.' Sam was sitting in the frowzy green and mauve armchair. 'Bet you'd love to palm my helmet...'

Out front they groaned.

Sam took the helmet from me and I tripped away downstage left, trying to undo my body armour. I had the Velcro straps arse about face.

'Please, can you help; you're nearest.' This to an officer sitting beside Colonel Curtis on the love seat.

'Certainly, dear lady.'

Out front, they cheered.

'Melton, who I told you about,' Colonel Curtis helpfully pointed out.

Colonel Melton was my height, blond, with a smiling-through-sadness expression (too much Patsy Cline?) and an imploded abdomen.

'Delighted,' he said. 'Truly.' He reached around me and was ineffectual with a Velcro strap.

'Faster – we've got fully burgeoning Tchaikovsky!'

'You've actually done it up incorrectly, this bit should—'

'Quick – we'll miss my flick-flacks!'

He yanked at one strap, I yanked at another; his yank was stronger. I fell, pinning him beneath me on the love seat.

Out front, they bellowed.

In the first six minutes of my set I got a big laugh with: 'Thumbs flat on my floating ribs, please, Colonel – this is ballet, not S&M.' Also, a shout of 'Fucking hell!' and long applause for the 32 pirouettes. Before something kicked off at the back of the venue.

Stacks, spluttering and swearing, was being propelled to the stage in a melee of Marines. He later said that he allowed his fellow Marines to throw him to me as really fighting back would have caused carnage.

'Here you go, sweetheart. Present for you! Wants to join in nicely.'

There was silence in the venue. Stacks stood at ease watching me. I didn't realise that standing at ease meant that a Marine was respectfully waiting. And I still don't know what he was waiting for. Prodding at his pecs, I asked, 'Are our muscles for use in warfare, or are they just for gay display?'

Out front, like a mechanic who's been asked for his thoughts on a clicking noise behind the glove box, they extravagantly sucked in air. Stacks grabbed me around the floating ribs and upended me. They cheered.

On my way tittuping chin first down Stacks's arse and legs to be laid out on the stage, I saw Nicky check in with Ian. Ian stood up. Colonel Melton made a 'hold fast' gesture at him.

Kneeling over me Stacks hissed, 'Where's your fucking zip?'

Reaching for it myself wasn't, on balance, clever. He got to it first.

'Stacks, no!' I shouted up from beneath his hamstrings.

'Not so fucking lippy now, are we, princess?'

He started unzipping the tutu.

'Stacks – don't seek, you may find.'

He thought about it, then picked me up off the floor, slung me over his shoulder and set off running.

'Belay!' Backing up a few steps, he hunkered down. 'Your body armour.' I picked it up. 'Para?' Sam, mouth open, handed me my helmet.

Past the ablutions, along the wire, across the now-deserted five-a-side pitch. A line of sun through the mountains was all that remained of daylight. Stacks muttering the whole way.

'My lot weren't meant to be here. The *fucks*. But they saw the CSE poster with you in your fluffy outfit on it. And expecting Royal Marines to stay away from a bit of drag is like expecting a politician to go for a colonic and not get a doggy bag.'

He tipped me off his shoulder and onto a tank.

'But that's no excuse,' he shouted up at me. 'This' – he pointed – 'is the *Naughty Tank*. But you're not staying up there for a minute for every year of your life – talking of which, put your body armour and helmet on, please. No, you can get down again when you've sung "Tom Bowling", like on *Victory*.'

'What, even with my kryptonite lungs?'

'Sing or stay up there. Your choice.'

> 'Here, a sheer hulk, lies poor Tom Bowling, The darling of
> our crew No more he'll hear the tempest howling For Death
> has broached him to.'

'Can't get down. Stacks! I sang, didn't I? Don't just walk off!'

Chapter Ten

Nicky and Ian were standing with Sam as I walked back across the five-a-side pitch carefully holding my tutu against my belly – I might be *in extremis*, but a ballerina must never have droopy tulle.

Nicky shook her head ruefully at me. 'Get ready for the off, hon.'

Sam made the mechanic's sharp-intake-of-breath noise. 'You were a tad lucky just then that the Marines were guests on our base. You gig at a base *run* by Royal Marines and say something like that, you'll get fucked onstage by him, making a point in front of his mates. Maybe take that as a warning, not a challenge.'

Pulling that stunt on me, Stacks, really?

Overkill, much?

Bloody vast bastard, handling chubster me like a sheet he was folding to put in an airing cupboard.

And what was that about the colonels leaving me to myself to try to fend him off?

And the other turns can stop it with these There-but-for-the-grace-of-God *smiles. I wasn't canned off. I wasn't so much as booed. Actually, I was getting huge laughs.*

And applause!

Then Marine stopped play.

I'm phoning the Geneva Convention.

During the helicopter flight Stacks sat low in his seat, eyes shut; feigning sleep, I suspected.

Nicky said, 'You must, *must* keep coming onstage wearing your body armour and falling into someone's lap.'

I nodded, watching, as the helicopter tilted, the lights of the cars flowing on the roads below. Where were the people in the cars going? Did they ever forget that their country was occupied? How much infrastructure was back in place down there? Would a camel do the same kind of damage to a car that a deer would?

I said, 'Though it's tricky to repeat something that's happened spontaneously and make it look like it's unrehearsed. On tour in 2003 it was always touch and go in Giselle's "Mad Scene", moving an audience to real tears while accidentally losing my pink cami-knickers.'

Stacks pointed me to the seat next to him at the front of the bus.

'I'm in big trouble,' I told Michelle.

She nodded, giving me an amused rather-you-than-me look.

'I warned you,' Stacks said. 'Leave me respected and in peace.'

'I didn't get you onstage; your Marines *put* you onstage.'

'You made the smart-arse remark.'

'You were trying to intimidate me with your towering scowling.'

'Should have left you on the cocking tank.'

I didn't answer.

He glanced at me. 'You scowling looks like a beaver with PMT.' I couldn't keep the smile back. 'Right. We're shaking hands and it's forgotten.'

As we drove, he sat looking out across the desert to the various fires burning, gaze flicking between them, as though he were making a comparison.

'Weird to hear you sing again,' he said, and made the sound of a bass pedal organ. 'You've got some lungs on you, give you that. And fuck me, you've got some spins on you. Don't you get dizzy? If you have to barf – surely you have done in the past? – how do you get your mouth down that low neckline?'

'What?'

'Marines on shouts in theatre or in training are encouraged not to soil their environment. When we barf, it's down the insides of our uniforms.'

Oh.

'Have you trained in ballet since you were little?'

'I was never little, Stacks. When my mother's waters were about to break, flood warnings were issued across three counties. If you mean "young", then the answer's no, I wasn't doing ballet. I was on tour singing with my country-and-western-singing dad. At municipal halls renamed El Paso for the night. For Dagenham Ford plant workers dressed as cowboys and Indians, calling their Cortinas the mule train before grabbing a metal tray to hit themselves on the head. Alcohol sold as "liquor" with a lot of pointing. I closed the first half of a bill. Aged four, dressed in a matching daffodil extravaganza, following a troupe of all-singing, all-dancing animal puppets featuring Ernie Emu, who belted out "Anything You Can Do, I Can Do Better" while Jessie Giraffe took her knickers off.'

'What did you sing?' Michelle asked.

'"Please Help Me".'

'Is this you trying to get your own back?' Stacks asked. 'Fobbing me off with rehearsed interview bollocks?'

'All true.' Just enhanced. 'I read in the *Victory* night itinerary that you're from a musical family yourself.'

He didn't answer for a few seconds, sitting alert like a hunting mongoose. 'My nan on my father's side,' he said, subsiding again. 'Church organist – until Good Friday-gate, that is.' He grinned. 'Nan was playing for the three-hour Devotions service. One hymn every hour on the hour. The churchyard gate was directly opposite The Fox and Hens. Between hymns she went over there for a cheeky bevvy. For the third hymn – "When I Survey the Wondrous Cross" – they had to carry her up into the organ loft. Left her there to sleep it off. She beer-snored right through Easter Saturday and into the Resurrection.' Hand tensed on the barrel of his rifle, Stacks watched a convoy of three Snatch Land Rovers pass us going in the opposite direction. 'And how did you get from the singing to the ballet?'

'I first saw ballet when I was eighteen – studying at Guildhall and working at Covent Garden as an usherette. I got hooked on dancing the ultimate prima-ballerina roles. Ex-ballerina Stella Beddard, my boss at Covent Garden, gave me proper lessons on the

Swan Queen every evening in the foyer when I'd counted my stem gingers. I was possessed! Pirouetting around the bust of Dame Nellie Melba, feather-preening up the Grand Tier staircase, miming lakes of my mother's tears in the downstairs ladies' cloaks. In the Crush Bar one night I collapsed in my prince-induced panic with the wrong foot under my ear, and had to have the St John Ambulance.'

'So, basically, you saw Darcey Bussell's Sugar Plum and decided to go giving it tiddle-iddle-thud in six dozen doilies, spouting a mix of Arabic and German, forcing some poor sod to – so to speak – clean and jerk you?'

'Pretty much.' Of course I had to ask him: 'If we'd been on a Marine-run base and I'd goaded you onstage, would you really have done something sexual to me?'

I'd tried to speak too quietly for Michelle to hear. When I looked sidelong at her, her expression gave nothing away.

'Probably,' Stacks said. 'Though maybe you're a bit too in with my ultimate boss.'

'The First Sea Lord?'

'Her Majesty. She ticked Sir Alan off for not letting you sing longer on *Victory*. Actually, second thoughts, no, I would have.'

'Why?'

'Because you mouthed off with a sexually challenging remark.'

'Doing anything to me would be gay.'

'It would be Marine.'

'There, onstage?'

'At least in a Marine-run base I could be sure there wouldn't be any of 2 Para near enough to get in a sneaky feel.'

Now it was his expression that was unreadable.

Back at the APOD, the sentry waved us down. Stacks slid the passenger-door window open.

'Message from the Dutch chaplain, sir. He wants to see the British entertainment civilians in his drop-in chapel.'

The Dutch chaplain, twentysomething with a ruddy face and

thick reddish-brown hair, was sitting in his drop-in chapel reading by torchlight.

'Lars Ton.' He stood up. 'I would have wished that you might have asked if you could borrow my chapel light to take away to your comedy performance.'

Spoons apologised. 'It was all a bit needs-must with our equipment stuck in the UK. There was no one around to ask. I did leave a note.'

Lars sighed. 'Yes, and I was surprised, I must say, to receive such a note.' He gestured around. 'I have no window in my chapel. I was almost in the dark during service this evening. No electric lighting fixtures. And we cannot budget for candles.'

'Really sorry, Father. I went into your chapel and saw the light...'

Lars's lips twitched with the beginnings of a smile. 'Then perhaps this regrettable incident has not been quite the lost cause.'

Outside the accommodation Stacks bid us goodnight. 'Pat on the back to each and every one of you.'

I went after him to apologise again.

'Mate, it's forgotten. Honourable enemy exchange.'

I asked, 'Did you get your scar in one of those?'

'No, sorry to disappoint you, I got it from my dad being a bit hasty taking the stabilisers off my kiddie bike. Oh, the bit in your act about the Russian partner being stuck at Heathrow? Say he's in D and V quarantine.'

'D and V?'

'Diarrhoea and vomiting.'

I made a mental note.

'You did good before you went to the bad. I thought you'd die on your fucking arse. Ropy choice of act to bring out here.'

'Well, at the time I auditioned CSE were being offered poetry workshops, maternal women to sit knitting and burlesque for *innocent delectation*.'

'For innocent delectation it's Bulgaria, renting a cabin that's to all intents and purposes a sauna and hot tub with non-essential living quarters attached. Plus hiring Kalashnikovs and dirty, *dirty* Eastern European escorts.'

'And for *non*-innocent delectation?'

He leered. 'Thailand. Lady boys. Pre-op, post-op, in the corridor on the surgical trolley.'

Chapter Eleven

It was Sunday. CSE had been out in Iraq for six days. Tuesday and Wednesday Stacks had been called away from the base to, as he had it, get stuck into a couple of skirmishes. He put a photo up on his Facebook page showing a huge, jagged impact: 'Me and Dutchy hit them with all this tonnage and they get out from under it laughing.' Meanwhile, on Tuesday I'd taken a tumble onstage in Umm Qasr. On Thursday a sumptuously beautiful Marine had snogged me during my kiss-of-life routine and at curtain-down invited me back to the Marines' billet for a group photo. Nicky Ness had ordered me straight onto the bus, seconded by Stacks, who had said to take that thwarted-teenager look off my face: I knew full well that *reservist* Marine hadn't said 'group photo', he'd said 'group *fuck*'. On Friday Rhod Gilbert, having previously hung fire whenever my set was discussed, had asked would I mind if he said something? Right, *right* then – and he was off: saying I should keep the line *Are our muscles for use in warfare, or just for gay display?* Right? And I mustn't gesture vaguely saying that my Colchester stalker was out there somewhere. Right? Right. Then I needed a more positive gag to get myself out of the kiss-of-life routine. Rhod's suggestion: *With Royal Marines, you can give them a choice of end…*

Stacks had spent the first part of Sunday at the internet café, messaging his fiancée, Kim, and his family and surfing Wikipedia. We were now under the awning drinking tea, my tour diary on the table beside him. He had agreed to vet it for military-speak.

'Just been Wiki'ing the Virgin Mary, chick,' he was saying. 'This way she's had over the years of appearing to peasant kids. One called Bernadette first, at Lourdes – and they built that holy water Center Parcs. The Virgin Mary also appeared in Portugal. Nobody gave a monkey's. But there've been quite a few other sightings. And I believe, because there's one detail that the kids all describe. And there was no Facebook or messaging or whatever, so they can't be comparing notes. And they describe this *whatever it is* in exact detail, all these kids, across continents and the centuries, and their descriptions all tally.' He paused, looking at me. 'And this *whatever* is the Virgin Mary's shoes. See, being little their eye level is closer to the shoes than the eye-line of a grown-up would be, say, if the heavenly host had ever thought through the PR of who the Virgin Mary might more usefully appear to – Hitler, Myra Hindley and most of the Popes. And it gives me great hope, chick. Because if on the other side you can get these shoes – and they're an off-white espadrille, apparently, with a back, little embroidered flowers to show off your instep, and a kitten heel – "O death, where is thy sting"?'

He cleared the tea things and opened my tour diary.

'Ha! We all panic-pack, chick. In the past I've bought one boxing glove, the TV remote and my mother's dressing gown. Comes from being in the right state of grace before a tour to either of the big two. We all go out the night before and agree to leave Harvester quietly when they ask us to after we've spooned apple sauce into a couple of Dutchy's crevices and shown the waiter.'

. Go anything *but* quietly from the queue in KFC when they chuck us out for what Rink-Dink's doing on his knees. Get on the Tristar in the morning hanging out of our arses from having got so blind mortal.' He was grinning, ruefully. 'How were you coming out your first morning?'

'Quiet. Oh, so *quiet*. Renting the other bedsits in my house are a German editor, a Danish church housekeeper and Bulgarians with a two-year-old. I had to go for my shock-awake cold shower by candlelight.'

'Pagan ceremony or haven't paid the bill?'

'Seventy-six-trombone bathroom extractor fan.'

He tapped a page. 'HESCO is a specific brand name of anti-blast wall. Like not all vacuum cleaners are Hoovers. Maybe just use the general term anti-blast? You're not meant to sound like you're actually in the services, knowing the jargon.'

Which reminded me. 'On the way to that first gig – the one

you scuppered – when the squaddie made us all tea and Ian asked for his with a cow and couple of Julies, the squaddie wasn't having it. Wouldn't let him use military speak.'

'Not wanted from civilians.'

'Ian was in the SAS.'

'Just their kind of meat-head.'

'And you're Jack Spratt-lean?'

'During my last physical it was recorded with hushed tones that my quad muscles had a perfect length-to-girth ratio.'

He read on. 'Never heard the ablution crappers described as "Lilliput Teflon".'

'How can someone fit in the cubicles, let alone sit down, if they're of muscular hue?'

'Houdini breathe in each time pre-crap. I have to go on special training before I come out here to bulk down: less weights when I'm doing regains.'

I suspected that, yet again, he was pulling my leg. 'Regains?'

'Climb back onto a rope suspended over the tank of water you've just (silly idea, if you ask me) jumped into wearing at least thirty-two pounds of equipment.'

'And that's *less* training? Than what?'

'Less *weights*, I said, not less *training*.' He told me that aside from regains the basic commando training comprised 9-mile marches in 90 minutes; 6-mile endurance treks across Woodbury Common via pipes, tunnels, wading pools and an underwater culvert, topped off with a 4-mile run back to base; Tarzan assault courses; death slides; 30-foot rope climbs.

'And all this training carrying all that weight?' I asked.

'Apart from gymnastics.'

'Good, that would be an aesthetic no-no. Imagine Olga Korbut on the balance beam wearing half a tank. And are your PE teachers the stereotypical shouty-loudy type?'

'Only if you're blatantly not trying. In training I was shit-scared of the crawl through the tunnel underwater, and I blacked out and had to be pulled through just short of the other end. And as I was coming round – no need for the fuckers to have slapped me that hard, I still maintain – I thought that was it: I'd be dropped from the course. And all I could think of was going around again. Got up and jogged for another try. Got stopped by the PE teacher – except we tend to call them physical training instructors – telling me that tomorrow would be soon enough for another go. Next day, I made it. Just. They'll pick you up when you've fallen down and your face is to the ground and you can't do any more, sling you in a Land Rover, give you another go. But they'll show you the door with a boot up you if you don't go all out at whatever bollock-ridden thing.'

'Why would you want to put yourself through it?'

'My dad was in the infantry, and my older brother followed him. Military family. It was really always a matter of me choosing my service. I watched a documentary on the Marines, and it looked a bit gruesome and a bit different, so eight years ago I signed on the dotted line.'

'Was there bloodshed in the documentary?'

'No, it was a training exercise. But this guy ran toward the camera looking as if he was about to die on his feet. When he was in close-up, he spilled his guts. Then smiled right into the camera.' He looked at me. 'Why are you putting yourself through this?'

'I'm poor. CSE pay.'

'All yours, or do you go through an agent?'

'I'm a variety artiste. Agents are as germane to us as sex education is to the cabbage-patch stork.'

'I can imagine you drive a hard bargain. I'm coming to see you as a bit like the member of the Gooch Gang who kept his pet baseball bat wrapped in a feather boa. And how are your family taking to you being out here?'

'Dad's having a breakdown, Mum's knitting you a balaclava.'

He riffled through pages in the diary. 'Where's the stuff about the camels? And the checkpoint at Smitty?' He imitated me. '"So sorry, Mr Policeman, but no driving licence with me in Iraq – or anywhere – because of the nasty instructor man; and my passport's under my second-best tutu. For ID can I show you my Sandcastle Casino membership?"'

'Might we please correct the military speak and jargon, and not the content?'

'Might we please keep our bonnet on, Emily Brontë? Name of the Thursday transport?'

The aeroplane in question had looked like the lovechild of Thunderbird 2 (finally!) and a basking shark. There were canvas seats with red webbing at their backs to hold onto. A stainless-steel privy was anything but private, in full view at the front right. The pipes, dial casings and all the rest of it were grey. It had been like sitting in an Airfix model. Embarkation and disembarkation via a ramp at the back. Up and down the shark's willy. We had had to kneel in rows before embarkation. In prayer that the big, bloated flying chubbster would get off the ground, I imagined.

'Hercules?' I ventured.

He nodded, then tapped the page. 'When I mentioned *Adobiran*, it wasn't a neighbouring country. A *Dhoby Run* is Marine-speak for doing laundry. Unless you're leaving your kit to percolate in your cat's piss. When did I take you to Death Valley and show you where the enemy hang our limbs off trees?'

'Artistic licence.'

'Otherwise known as lies – or something you were told by a Para. Let alone that Death Valley's in Korangal, *Afghanistan*. Same as the Himalayas you've described four times and counting.'

He was clearly unhappy with my mention of Death Valley. I promised to cut it.

When he handed the diary back, he said, 'All present and correct, passed by the censor. Just watch stuff added for sensationalism, like the bit about Death Valley. Mind-fuck, seeing your mates desecrated in that way. Private matter, not... not...' He drummed with his palms on his thighs. 'What's it called when desk jockeys discuss something they've seen on TV?'

'Water-cooler chat.'

Chapter Twelve

CSE were sitting on the bus waiting for Stacks's understudy. Stacks had flown to Qatar for the day on a promise of champagne, silk sheets and shenanigans. I hadn't asked if Kim was flying out for a conjugal visit. I suspected not.

'Oh, Lordy, this'll be fun for you all,' said Michelle.

'It's the Brecon Beacons in combats,' Rhod said.

'Regimental Sergeant Major Ayres,' Michelle said.

Something caught RSM Ayres's eye. 'What the—?' he said in a muffled roar, making a detour to the anti-blast wall and plucking off it my newly tea-dyed ballet tights. He climbed onto the bus. 'Whose?'

'Mine. Best place to dry them after they've been in the tea.'

'We are in a military outpost of vital significance to the current war effort, not a laundromat for West End Wendy's wash-to-wear.'

He nodded at Michelle.

'Sir,' she said.

He looked like a St Bernard that had had work done. Eyes like blue tinsel. Standing on the bottom step leaning against the front passenger seat, the top of his head still reached the roof of the bus.

'Need to keep my back straight,' he explained.

'For the sake of high status,' Nicky whispered.

'Or lumbago,' Andy whispered back.

'I am RSM Ayres. Known as Pam. Anyone want to laugh? No? Good. While our hugely esteemed Lieutenant Osborne is—'

'Who?' Rhod asked.

'Stacks.'

'While our esteemed Lieutenant Osborne is up north ridding himself of his current blue-of-bollock state, I am looking after you.' His sinuses appeared to be fluttering. 'Unstinting goodness of heart. First things first: I don't like paperwork, so don't get killed on my watch.' He looked at Michelle with a sneer. She stared straight ahead. Shrugging, he went on, 'For the duration of today's whatchamacallit I shall be gadding you folks about.' Even allowing for the Lancashire accent, he must intentionally have pronounced folks as 'fucks'. 'The aforementioned whatchamacallit is to be out at Basra Palace. After which gad, I shall be gratefully handing you *back* to the aforementioned Lieutenant Osborne. I'm not interested in any of your art or your self-PR. My brief is simply to keep the fuckers over the wire from curtailing your time roaming this troubled planet.'

He paused.

'Fucking hell!' Andy said.

'I will, for your sake, take that expletive as a compliment. Michelle... shall we?'

Michelle gunned the engine and drove to the gate.

'What the fucking fuck... !' Pam shouted. He vaulted from his seat and off the bus.

We watched as he reached the sentry box in two steps and began cuffing it.

'Are we sitting in there reading and not watching?' Biff. 'Reading in-fucking-there, are we?' Another biff.

'Not any more, he isn't,' said Rhod, as the duty guard emerged like a reluctant badger.

'Give,' Pam bellowed. The duty guard handed him a copy of *Viz*. 'Fuck you, lad, and fuck your un-fucking-suitable reading matter. Having to pick up every last shred will at least bring you from sitting there in your box out into the open, where you might catch sight of something that's liable to happen in a war zone such as the one – you seem to be forgetting – we're in at the moment!'

He tore the copy of *Viz* to confetti.

At the airport Pam got off the bus to oversee the CSE equipment being loaded into the helicopter, and we huddled around Michelle.

'What's his story, Michelle?' Spoons asked.

She wound up the driver's side window. 'Ex-Guardsman—'

'Figures,' Ian said. 'We always say when we do gigs for Guards:

get on the stage, get on with the job and get the hell out of there and leave them to their lairyness.'

'Fonteyn always said that about performing *Swan Lake* in Paris.'

'He appeared on *The Generation Game*.'

'Demonstrating cream-puff piping?'

'The Georgian gliding dance?'

'Cuddly toy?'

'Square bashing,' said Michelle. 'The producer asked him not to tone his voice down just because he was in a TV studio but to give it the full welly. Imploded two banks of speakers.'

'CSE!' we heard bellowed. 'CSE!' It was Pam, beckoning. We got off the bus. 'Your presence is required on board the helicopter. Obey instructions with no shilly-shallying.' He waved at Michelle, who saluted before shifting the bus gears to reverse for a three-point turn. 'That turn weren't bad for a woman.' He led us around the anti-blast wall. 'This is where they would give you the talk about not getting too close to that evil-looking tail propeller. But you just feel free to lessen my burden and walk straight at it. I jest. You hope.'

During the flight out to Basra Palace, Pam, nearest the evacuation ramp, stared at each member of the CSE tour for half a minute or so. Or nodded off. Or got up from his seat to look out of a porthole.

'That's the situation in Iraq sorted now,' Nicky shouted in my ear. 'Just from one of his Paddington Bear stares.'

On landing, he hustled us across the airstrip. 'Clear the landing area, quick, quick, quick! The helicopter and crew need to get away sharpish, being as they are on a schedule. Twinkle, twinkle, twinkle!'

We twinkled to the front entrance of the palace, where Pam turned to watch the helicopter taking off again.

'You are blessed to be transported on such a piece of kit – and, as civilians, should be truly thankful.'

I asked, 'Is there a mode of transport we can go by that civilians never normally would?'

Pam cupped his hands, fingertips together to form an S-bend, as though he were about to recite.

'How about...

'... I put you...

'... in a tank...

'... and drive it...

'... through the walls of Basra bollocksing Palace?'

Talking – no, *bawling* – of which, he patted the section of wall the allies' tank had smashed through in 2003. 'Haven't they made a quality job of the shoring up?'

'And took less than three years,' I said. 'When my aunt made the hole in the church wall, driving my nan to the bookies – her brakes failed, but she couldn't just turn right at the foot of Church Hill and freewheel the car to a stop because she'd explained things to my nan, who promised not to panic, but still put the steering wheel in a choke-hold, screaming they were going to die and she wasn't sure she had clean pants on – it took Bargoed Council fifteen years to refill.'

Pam was still in his recital pose. 'Then just as well the MOD doesn't outsource building deployment to the Llantyllangogogoch Ranting Druid Circle Construction Company with their wattle and daub, flint hammers and however many choruses as it takes of "Men of Harlech".' He stroked the shored-up plaster approvingly. 'Inside, please.'

We walked beneath a portico arch supported by pillars, flanked by bay windows, in colours ranging from soft to liver pink. Inside was a central dome of recessed honeycomb and half-moon wedges, decorated in foliate arabesque. The liver pink was repeated here, with chrome yellow and turquoise.

Beneath the dome the Seven Armoured Brigade CO waited to greet us. Tall and grey with cataracts in the early stages, he got as far as saying: 'Good evening, thank you for coming out here—' and he, CSE and all were swept aside by Pam's monologue. 'Sir, CSE artsome wasters, you're most likely thinking. I imagine they'll want to see where they'll be prancing and cavorting in case everything's not as their artsome little hearts would desire it; and then will want to fill their artsome faces. No, you're not an artsome. He's on the technical side, sir. Known as Spoons, the wherefore and the why of which I can't say. Some bodies, Spoons? Being where we are and under the duress which we are, I should have phrased my request for lifting and carrying assistance with a sprinkling of the magic dust that comes courtesy of the Tact Fairy.'

The CO excused himself. Pam looked wistfully after him for a few seconds, then jabbed open a door. 'Your so-called Green Room. Once a meeting place for Saddam and his dastardly doings. I hope to see you truly thankful for that which you are about to receive.' A buffet was laid out. There was also a pool table, cabinets, a blank A-board and some tatty armchairs. 'Might have been Saddam's his very self's, yon chairs. Oh, now, if you please, turns, not such a rush to park on such relics of historical wrongdoing thy beleaguered bot-bots.'

Laying out what I needed for the show, I asked Pam where I might find a needle and thread.

'Are you about to become unstuffed?'

'I need to darn my left ballet shoe.'

He spluttered. 'Darn-my-left-ballet-shoe. Did I hear you correctly? *Darn-my…* I shall stoop to ask at the hospital, but shouldn't think they'll want to assist with something so untowardly quee… frilly. Turns, comport yourselves with decorum, try to, till I get back.'

Tonks said, 'Good move, Iestyn. Everyone else: for sanity's sake, think of errands to send him on.'

'Should have sent him for whole cards of needles for the frogs to count,' I said, referring to the *Tale of Foolish John*. 'And for the cloth. And the bales of thread to twine around the cloth to keep the gum tree warm while the frogs are counting the needles.'

'Shaves… shaves!' An Iraqi in a navy blue dishdasha and tan brogues stood smiling at a side door. 'I am Ali. I do nice work for British, Americans, Canadians. In my uncle's shop in town before and now I come here.' He sidled into the room. 'Shaves. And I play pool very good.'

'Then put 'em up, Ali,' said Andy.

'Fuck off out of here, you!' It was Pam bellowing from the doorway, holding a gingham huswife. Ali slotted his pool cue back into the rack and bolted.

'Turns, there are signs on all the doors leading in and out of this Green Room specially set aside for you that its use is for nobody but yourselves, myself or officers. Your needle and thread, Mr Edwards. On-duty nurse allowed me to bring this to you on one condition: that you go and visit them in what she politely termed your full rig. So, think on and be prepared. Time waits for no man... in your case I use the term "man" so loosely, it's verging on the prolapsical.'

'Iestyn.' It was Spoons at the door that led from the Great Hall. 'Come and look at the stage.'

It was wrought iron, standing about 3 feet high, a foot and a half across. A gully ran down its centre, flanked by two curved ridges. I could barely manage to stand on it. 'Is it something for me to be propelled along at the behest of a supercriminal toward a laser beam that has my willy's name on it?'

A Scouse voice from the back of the hall said, '*Goldfinger*. Except the laser moves and 007 stays put. Tied up.'

A very ripped squaddie in a white vest and blue tracksuit bottoms was bullying a screen along behind the seating. He checked that it was dead centre beneath the vaulted ceiling and steadied it on its feet, turning it through 45 degrees. A painting was mounted on the screen.

'Lambsy. Guardsman.' We shook hands. There was a callous on his palm like a plague sore.

The painting was of Lambsy wearing a personal stereo and a pea-green pouch, posing *most muscular* in the shallows of a lake. Meanwhile, an amphibious vehicle was coursing through deeper water and heading straight for him.

'That's me in the picture, out for my run,' Lambsy explained, unsmiling, tapping the painting. 'You'll see that I'm wearing a Walkman. You won't hear that I'm listening to Def Leppard. The vehicle', he tapped the picture again, 'was returning from patrol. I didn't hear it until it was right smack behind me. Unfortunately, becoming aware of it, I misjudged which side of me it was on, as well as thinking it was closer than it was, and on the spur of the moment jumped the wrong way. Into the water. At the exact same time as I jumped the driver made a split-second decision and turned right. If he had turned left, I would have been certainly mowed underwater. I got away with only a hell of a dead leg off the wave buffeting me.' He tapped the picture a third time. 'It's the lads' funny story going around – has been since it happened.'

'When was that?'

'Five months, three weeks ago. It was still hot enough weather then for me to wear something that skimpy.'

I turned the painting so that it would face the incoming audience. 'You haven't made yourself nearly big enough.'

Lambsy tried so hard not to smile he nearly dislodged his moustache.

'For the one who sows to his own flesh will from the flesh reap corruption,' Pam's voice came booming from the door to the hall. 'Note how the high ceiling gives such marvellous amplification. I warrant that'll be vital for what I should think will be you lot's level of laughter.'

'Sir,' said Lambsy as Pam approached.

Pam, looking from Lambsy to the screen and back again, said, 'Are you the person represented in this art work?'

'Sir.'

'There's clearly not enough for you to do.'

'Sir.'

'Is there anything else you could be getting on with at the present moment?'

'Yes, sir.'

'Then I suggest you go and get on with it. We don't want a

decent British soldier catching airy-fairyness from the wilfully art-some.'

'Sir.' Lambsy turned to walk away.

I said, 'Pam, talking of the wilfully artsome: how did you over-shout on *The Generation Game*?'

'My quite exquisite demonstration of square bashing?' He stared slightly rheumy-eyed at me.

'Yes. Curious.'

'Then, as and when you do something warranting the required degree of outrage, you shall find out.'

Lambsy, on his way out of the hall, said, 'Oh, fuck, not clever.'

Back in the Green Room I put my hand down the leg of my newly dyed ballet tights to stretch them – and, well now, how right Stacks had been: you did get a better finish in the nylon with loose leaves.

I was telling Tonks about Lambsy and the painting for him to use as material when Pam slammed into the Green Room and charged at me.

'Who is responsible for this area here?' he shouted, jabbing his finger in the direction of first my tutu, then my tights and then at each item of make-up in turn.

'Er... me,' I said.

'Pink... frills... slut's devices... Looks like a gypsy en-fucking-campment. Tidy it up! Before I get back! And your milk-bottle-white legs. Lose them. We currently find ourselves in a beautifully administered military outpost. Not the Prestatyn Sands Pontins. Put on long trousers! Put on long trousers!! Long trousers!!! Put on!!!! PUUUUUUUUUUUTTTTTTTTTT!!!!!'

His exit fell just this side of being pure Max Wall.

A wind had risen, skimming a top layer off the sand as I went to visit the hospital togged up in my pinks and frills. I was thinking Mother Teresa, Princess Diana, American soprano Clara Louise Kellogg receiving the lock of hair from the Confederate soldier with the message: 'Tell her, as I die beneath this protecting oak, that I would not try to meet her; but that I have loved her, before God, as well as any man ever loved a woman.'

I could only wave and shout a greeting from out in the corridor, the one patient in the hospital being in diarrhoea-and-vomiting quarantine.

'They lied to you,' Pam said. 'He's actually got a mild flesh wound. But I forewarned them that with your proclivities, you'd insist on administering a bed bath.'

He was daintily choosing things from the buffet and arranging them on a paper plate. Out in the venue Tonks worked up to introducing Rhod. I sat in one of the armchairs to warm up my feet, going from tiptoe to flat and back up.

'Iestyn, that big guy Lambsy,' Andy said. 'He was apprenticed to his mum in her hairdressing salon, but got a bellyful of the constant piss-taking and signed up to be a Guardsman. Now wishes he hadn't. Just wants to be back on the Wirral with his adjustable chair and his layering scissors and "Do you want some gel or wax on that?" I could tell just now he was about to bawl.'

'Pray silence', Pam interrupted, sitting down with a hanky spread over his knees, 'for this breaded prawn!' About to take a first bite he looked over at me.

'What now?' I asked.

'You doing St Vitus's dance in that chair.' He put the prawn and hanky aside, stood and began to circle the chair, sliding his hand under the arms and along the joint at the back.

'What?'

'Just checking that this chair isn't a Saddam special. If it were and you sat there with your toes a-going in the full Ginger Rogers manner you might set off the mechanism. In this very room would Saddam, feigning innocence, invite a traitorous minion to take a pew. And, in a flash, leather tentacles would have pinioned their limbs. Then think of it as an ice-cream sandwich: you'd be the vanilla in the middle, the sides of the chair would be the wafers. And Saddam would flick a switch and the wafers would move in on the ice-cream squeezing tighter and tighter until vanilla-you would be turned to raspberry-coulis-you, all oozing and red and lumpen. And what did I say to you first off on the bus this morning? That's right: "Don't get killed on my watch."'

The wind was really up now, throwing the sand about. Making out a canal bridge in the blackout, I remembered Stacks telling how the insurgents had been using bits of bedstead as rocket launchers. I turned my head toward the slatted metal wall and lurched my way to the back door to the venue. Tilting my tiara up (not clever, as it turned out), I put my ear to the door to listen for my music cue. It came, I opened the door, and just then the wind whipped around behind me and blew me head-first through it. There was huge applause as I face-planted in the CSE backdrop. My already skew-whiff tiara now hung from my hairnet. I tried to jam them back on and caught sight of Pam at the back of the venue. He looked outraged. I danced on, regardless.

I threw my tiara onto the pile of slut's devices and reached for my wet wipes. 'That wasn't so bad with the stage, after all.'

'I wouldn't know,' said Pam, helping himself from the buffet. 'Watching your perverted antics would sully my retinas and delicate sensibilities.'

'You were watching at the back, Pam.'

'Wishful thinking. And if you wouldn't mind keeping your airing of narcissism to yourself, I'd like to enjoy a quiet moment with these pineapple chunks. And we've a helicopter to catch in seven minutes and counting down. I'd advise the getting on of a wriggle.'

Leaving my tutu on under my body armour, I wore my sweater as a shawl so as not to break the helicopter flight rule (No Bare Arms) and clipped the tiara into the housing on the side of my helmet. I was first out of the palace door into the blackout. I could hear the helicopter approaching and made for the runway.

'Mr Edwards, come back here, please...'

I kept walking, not wishing just then to be a stooge in the *Pam Show*. The helicopter was getting closer.

'Mr Edwards, slow down…'

And closer still. I kept walking. I was making a point here.

'Mr Edwards!'

There was a white flash near my feet. I looked down and could just make out the glow of the cross marking the centre of the helicopter landing area. I took a breath to say, 'Oh shit…', and heard: 'Mr Edwards, I'd get off there, if you don't want to be wearing that fucking helicopter!'

I ran, reaching the others in safety, turning to watch the helicopter touch down right where I'd just been. Pam was chuntering about how grateful he would be to hand us back to Stacks – 'Mentioning no names specifically, of course' – then nodded permission for us to make for the helicopter.

I said, 'Pam, there's a blackout: how could you see me?'

'Landing lights glinting off your tiara.'

Chapter Thirteen

Stacks had his head on one side, appraising me. We were in a mess bar back in the APOD compound. 'Just seeing what kind of reception I'm getting taking you back from Pam.'

I opened a can of lager. 'Jury's out.'

'Bit like when my nan got back from her holidays and collected the dog from the kennels. Let's wait and see if you stage a dirty protest in your food bowl; scoot yourself everywhere suckering the floor with your bum hole; or get on the piano specially to give us a flash of dwarf salami rampant.'

Enthroned on a bar stool a few beers later, Pam said to me, 'I'm homophobic, and I admit to it. But I've taken a shine to you, young man.'

'You've known me one day.'

'A day lived with death sees time condense.' He made a shushing gesture at me and everyone went quiet. 'You've needed sharp keeping in order and perhaps I may have overegged the pudding. I esteem you. Lowly, not highly, but I esteem you.'

'And I still want you to arrange for us to have that ride in a tank.'

In a truly outstanding bass baritone he sang me the obscene version of the 'Eton Boating Song' – 'I sold my Ford to a man at Sissinghurst, He asked what was my bottom price, I said, At least buy the car first' – followed by 'Two Little Boys'.

No rising in his chest, textbook expansion in his lower ribs, the massive St Bernard head giving his voice startling natural resonance. There was a moment of gobsmacked silence, then long applause.

Pam nodded, looking at nobody. 'I am quite the reticule of entertainment.'

Later, I asked Pam about Lambsy admitting to being terrified out in Iraq. 'You probably went and gave him a smack and told him to pull himself together?'

'You mean the budding Van Gogh?' He shook his head. 'I fully understand him being terrified. Though we have the best trained army in the world and are relatively well equipped, nothing ever prepares an individual for a conflict. My first ever shout – South Armagh: we were mortared, shot at, burnt out, blown up. We were alien people in alien surroundings with very few, if any, friends outside that wire. Not to mention I had diarrhoea like a flock of bats in freefall.' He tapped his forefinger on the bar. 'The vast majority of the men and women who are involved out here are young, with little or no experience of these types of operations. They grow up fast. Him you mentioned actually showed some mettle because he dared get his feelings out into the open. And his feelings would be echoed by a good many more out here if they could be so honest. So, no, I wouldn't have gone and given him a slap and told him to buck his ideas up.'

He added, 'Though I'm not quite finished with you, think on. All is not forgiven.'

'Shake a collective leg, vaudevillians,' Pam bawled, waking us at six the next morning. He swatted aside our obscenities. 'And prepare to be truly grateful. I have arranged with a quite overwhelmingly kind tank battalion to let you have that ride in one of their vehicles. And you' – he meant me – 'here's a little present. It's a desert scarf. Official issue. Last night at Basra Palace coming onstage with your tiara knocked all to hell and back was a disgraceful want of professional decorum. Don't you fob me off with a tale told of a sandstorm! What did I say about this not being a holiday camp? You're out in the desert in winter. I never promised you a go on the dodgems, a stick of rock and a paddle with your trousers rolled up to your pudgy, pale knees. You put this scarf over your head-furniture as you're about to go onstage, nothing will be dislodged. Even in a mortar attack there'd be no movement whatsoever from a full set of heated curlers. And, furthermore, apropos of your near run-in with that helicopter, the scarf will provide a portable blackout.' He tilted his head back and looked past his nose, beyond me, smiling complacently at the scarf. 'And if you should misguidedly feel the need to embroider it, please use something appropriately plain and militaristic, like cross stitch.'

Our last show of the tour was in the Basra NAAFI. My onstage warrior was Reggie, a nineteen-year-old Highlander, tank regiment. Lanky and with a grin wide enough to pierce his cheekbones, Reggie jumped so high he smacked his head on a light – one of Spoons's official kit lights, which had arrived just that morning from Brize Norton in time for this last show.

'Iestyn, I'm away down to Shaibah.' Stacks was holding out a slip of paper. 'My contacts. Safe journey home. Whenever that may be. Tristar left Brize four hours behind schedule. CSE probably won't be able to get on it when it does come. Lads going home on R and R have precedence.'

We hugged. He smelt of Joop and fresh laundry.

'Maybe catch up with you in KAF? CSE tends to get something out there around May time.' Seeing my puzzled look he explained: 'KAF's Kandahar, in your money.' Then he was walking away, eyes front while mine clouded over.

CSE did in fact get on the Tristar. Already four hours late, it was delayed a further six hours in Basra while a landing light was repaired. Looking up every so often from my book, I saw, in stop-motion, two Royal Irish Regiment boys asleep on the floor change position until they were spooning. Other members of the regiment pointed down at them with 'Those two!' smiles.

In the early hours a bomb-seeking robot jerked its way into the hangar.

'Oh, fuck…'

It stopped.

'This is not looking good…'

Stuck in the sensor arm at the front was a note. The Royal Irish squaddie nearest gingerly pulled it out.

'This is for you comedians.'

The note read, 'Cheers for coming out here to entertain us!!! Lol xXx.'

Due to the exigencies of onward postings for the Royal Irish and Highlanders regiments, the Tristar stopped off in Hanover (I rang my father), Birmingham and Scotland. In all that return trip took twenty-three hours.

Oh my word, safe.

And I have some nice money.

Didn't get canned off. Tonks admitted to me that he and everyone thought I'd die on my arse, and he had to say I stormed the gigs. Don't remotely agree with that, but it was nice to hear it said.

Wasn't in the slightest bit chewed by a camel spider.

Only really got seriously scared out on the road that day.

When my Camden Library card wouldn't cut it…

So content with time slowed to just sit here, safe, going home.

Please let Stacks stay safe.

All the sudden *colour* everywhere. Back in St Pancras, I trod caked Iraqi dirt all up the stairs and across the carpet in my bedsit. I couldn't bear to Hoover it up for over a week.

There was a message from my stepmother. 'Oh, thank you, *thank you* for the phone call. He was so relieved when he heard it we had some tears.'

And one from my mother: 'Oh, right, yes. Just wondering when you were back from *you-know-where*, which of course I can't say out loud just in case… security. Sophia's sister says she's taken to locking the kitchen door when she goes to the pub on Friday because she's heard that the *you-know-what* are planning to invade.'

Walking to Sainsbury's in Camden, I had flashbacks to the tank ride, desert skies, dirty-sand tents with uniforms strung up to dry between them. Friends, when I rang to catch up, told me that I would need so much time to process my experiences. The violence. The otherness.

The Pam...

> Iestyn my mate, how nice to get your email. And you're more than welcome! I just hope you're wearing said precious gift. You are truly barking as a turn and I don't know how you do it, particularly where you've just been. I was surprised to say the least when I heard what you were to be about. But I suppose you have little choice but to carry on with it because of the scarcity of Rest Homes for Retired Sugar Plums. I heard talk they're planning on sending you to Afghanistan. What a hankering they seem to have for sending you to the front line in a frock. If you were to catch a bullet, I think our main worry is how would we describe what you are for the death certificate? We'd get into trouble from the PC lot writing you're an obese, homo, black swan – yes, black swan, by the end with all that muck on your tutu.

> Thank you for your kind information that I have been mentioned in interviews you've given to the *Mail on Sunday*, *The Times* and whatever *Full House* magazine may be. I would, however...
>
> RATHER READ THE FUCKING BEANO!!!
> Take care, kid. Best... Pam.

Pam dominated my interviews for *The Times*, the *Mail on Sunday*, and *Full House*.

The Times, for whatever reason, cut my references to camels and custard creams; the *Mail* replaced my gibbering panic with me strutting around quoting the Duke of Wellington; *Full House*, whose summer issue containing my article would be out in May, didn't correct my assumption that it was a theatre-trade rag.

'And because you are a dedicated theatre publication,' I had said, 'I feel I can tell you all about the creative process behind Madame Galina…'

Stacks, meanwhile, was taking a mock proprietorial stance to my Iraq experiences.

'Exactly how much of a special mention will Pam be getting in your… come again: *my* book?' he messaged one Sunday. 'I want the opening line. Chapter one, paragraph one, line one – mention of me.'

I reminded him that CSE needing to be shunted around by Pam had been his own doing, but did include some suggestions for the opening line of his book.

Last night I dreamt I went to Marine Base Lydd again…

Call him Stacks…
    It was a dark and stormtroopery night…
    It was the Stacksiest of times, it was the age of Stacks, it was the epoch of Stacks, it was the season of Stacks…
    It is a truth universally acknowledged that a drag ballet act sent to entertain in the deserts of Iraq must be in want of a knockabout, shouty, balding Royal Marines Commando…

'Belay! Don't tell them I'm going bald. I'm hating losing my hair.'

'It's the testosterone.'

'It's my age.'

'I have noticed that the skin's just beginning to knit at the back of your neck, just above where the muscle bulges. I can imagine you in a few years, wearing a wife-beater, bucket hat and ankle tag, eating picked eggs, extorting with menaces, always being kind to your Great Aunty Vi.'

'Christ up a fucking pole.'

'Embrace your age, Stacks. Would the butterfly want to be the caterpillar again? The swan the ugly duckling? The chicken the egg… the egg the chicken… the chicken… ?'

'Finished? You'd have loved me even more – I know, not possible! – if you'd seen me with major hair. If worst came to worst, I'd want it down in big writing on my death notice that I still had Christopher Robin curls.'

'Don't you mean obituary?'

'That's for famous people. The rest of us get a death notice.'

'What's the difference?'

'A paper can choose whether or not to include a celeb's obituary. The undertaker pays the paper to put a death notice in for Joe Bloggs as part of the funeral package. Think of a famous murder case where the victim wasn't a known somebody…'

'The Borden case.'

'Bet you in the same paper there was a blue-murder headline and a hushed-tones death notice.'

The *Fall River Herald*'s headline ran: 'A Venerable Citizen and His Aged Wife HACKED TO PIECES IN THEIR HOME!' Tucked away in the births, deaths and marriages pages was: 'Died in her home at 92 Second Street, Fall River, Mass., on August 4th 1892, Abby D. Borden, second wife of Andrew Borden, age 65; also died at eleven o'clock at the same time and place, Andrew Borden, aged 70.'

'See, chick, when you get the headline on the newsstand about the however many-eth squaddie killed in Iraq or Afghanistan, there'll be a local paper somewhere with a death notice in the classifieds: "Beloved son of…" or "Faithful husband of…" or "Adored father of…"'

'"Adored wife or mother or sister of"?'

'Much rarer, statistically. And female personnel's deaths are most often suicides from Post-Traumatic Stress Disorder. So, you will only tend to see the "Adored son/father/husband of…" And in my case: "Adored fiancé…"'

Part Two

Part Two

Chapter Fourteen

On a May Monday, Nicky Ness rang. 'Afghanistan Friday, please, hon.'

It was more a command than a request.

I had torn my right hamstring Easter Saturday dancing a solo as the Queen of Hearts in an *Alice* installation, and even now – three weeks or so later – it still killed. I couldn't *relevé*, *fouetté* or bunny hop, and the back of my right leg looked like mashed canaries. I really ought to have said no.

I spent the rest of the day creating a disaster zone in my bedsit finding my passport.

There has never been, isn't now and never shall be a suitable gap behind that gilt mirror.

Oh, that's *what that smell has been.*

Excellent, my spare feathers.

Second time of telling re: the gilt mirror.

Why is there a Christmas bauble in the spillover cutlery drawer?

Oh, for the love of all things, this is a one-open-space bedsit, not the umpteen stateroom, corridor and vestibule Palace of Versailles.

Not behind the gilt mirror, third time, really!

'But from what original amount do you want your round number of dollars?'

Friday had come and I was jelly-brained with fear at the Bureau de Change counter, running late for the train to Oxford.

'The nearest one that will make a round number of dollars,' I answered.

'Approximately?'

'Can I not have it exactly?'

'You need to tell me how many pounds you'll be giving me to start with.'

The cent dropped. 'Sixty?'

How incongruous for a bus to go from the dreaming spires to somewhere so desolate as the Brize Norton airfield. I wondered if I would see Stacks in Afghanistan. In early March he had sent me some photos taken on his grandparents' farm: 'Premature lambs in the warming oven of the Aga AWWWWWW, princess, look!!!'

At 2am one Sunday morning he had rung from a club in Canal Street. 'Princess, tell this girl, Sophie, that you're writing a book all about me. Trying to pull her. Putting you on speakerphone, chick.'

A female voice had asked, 'So is he not spinning me a line here, then?'

'It's mainly about him, but there are other people in it.'

I was quick-smarted back off speakerphone. 'Other people?' Stacks hissed in mock fury. 'What part of "trying to pull" here did you miss? Mentioning other fucking people. TUBBIN!'

TUBBIN – Marine-speak for 'thumb up bum brain in neutral'.

Any softening influence I might have had on him out in Iraq, I suspected, must have worn off by now. In spite of our jokey communicado, I tended to picture him unsmiling, taking and giving orders in full warry mode, flinty and aggressive.

When the bus stopped at Brize Norton the only other passengers were two elderly ladies. They seemed so concerned as I got down, I felt I should reassure them that I was only going out to Afghanistan to entertain.

One said, 'Yes. We were thinking that the very last thing you looked was soldierly.'

I met Ian again, Colin Cole, who was the compère on this tour, and Phil Butler. Ian, watching my feet as I approached, asked if I was walking okay. I explained about the hamstring injury, and how four times daily, on physio's orders, I was applying Voltarol to it and walking up hills. 'Will there be hills for me to use out in Afghanistan?'

'The Himalayas have been known to be quite hilly.'

Phil I knew from the circuit. He gathered me into an expensive-smelling hug, then let me check his bald head for closeness of shave. Colin was in his fifties, wearing black tracksuit bottoms and a T-shirt emblazoned with a photo of himself in younger, as yet ungrizzled days. Close to being 7 feet tall, the very largest-issue body armour looked like a child's size on him. Gazing around departures he said, '"Abandon hope all ye who enter" – or what?'

I got in the midst of some Paras. One said that he didn't recognise me not wearing my dress and another commented, 'Well, clearly you just did, you silly cunt.' He asked me if I was with the entertainments people.

I nodded.

'Any girls?' He was blond and shivering.

'I play a girl.'

'You'll do.'

Spoons, overhearing as he arrived carrying coffee and a pastry, commented, 'My grandfather was master of that kind of mysterious absolute.'

On the Tristar I sat in an aisle seat, so I could keep my hamstring stretched out as much as possible, and slept for most of the flight. Ian woke me for food and, once we were in Afghani airspace, to put on my body armour. As the blacked-out Tristar wove its way down into Kandahar airport Colin shouted, 'Jesus Christ, is there a woman flying this thing?' Then, as we taxied to arrivals he advised everyone not to relax just yet. 'She might realise she's left her mules in the warming oven and we'll be back up in the air any second.'

Threatening heat hit as we walked down the airstairs in the charred desert night. An officer was waiting for us. Dark curls, an oval face, clear liquid gaze – and how could he bear to wear his uniform scarf in this heat?

'CSE, welcome to Afghanistan. Major Whippen-Bedsoe: call me Rupert. Bit of the usual hurry up and wait.' His speech was almost foppish.

'Usual smell,' said Phil. 'Burning and petrol.'

Colin said, 'Let's pray they never get too close.'

I sat next to Spoons on the bus. Rupert climbed aboard, patted the driver's shoulder and said, 'Terminal.'

'That's a nice positive attitude to start a tour off with,' Spoons said as the bus set off, skirting the runway.

We pulled up at the holding bay, in a gravel clearing dotted with Portaloos and bucket ashtrays.

'Keep one ear on what's going on inside the hangar,' Rupert said. 'Info on on-goings shortly. Have a smoke those who want to go to hell in that particular way.'

Inside the hangar, non-smoker squaddies sat on spindly wooden benches watching Sky Sports. Ian took a CSE head count and nodded at a fridge, a sign on which read: 'One Cold Bottle Out, One Warm In'. I took out one cold and put in three warm from the box beside the fridge, saying a prayer for indulgence.

Ian said, 'In this heat: Pee-pale.'

'Do you check?' Colin wondered.

Rupert announced, 'All use of mobile phones out in theatre is forbidden. Don't so much as be seen with one. For Kabul, report here to desk H. For Kajaki to desk A. If you're staying here in Kandahar, look busy or I'll find you something to be getting on with.'

We made our way to desk H and Colin asked Rupert why we were forbidden to use mobiles.

'Death threats being made to people at home. Enemy sympathisers have been locking onto signals of calls being made to and from bases out here. I'm overdosing on ginseng and oysters and putting my ex-wife on pocket-speed-dial.'

Manning check-in – a free-standing wooden booth – was a squaddie who was powerful in the chest, with black gelled hair and a slightly slow left eye. A bald late-teen was leaning on the booth, asking, 'How can it not have got here by now, Turkish? It got sent a fortnight ago. I've had nothing for the whole of my tour.'

'I don't control how quickly the stuff gets here from home, Farnsey,' Turkish answered. 'And I don't put anything personal on priority.'

'What's in those sacks over there?'

'Maybe your parcel, but the system says we can't go rooting through them all.'

They had reached an impasse, Turkish with his palms raised, Farnsey shoulders sunk. Farnsey sighed heavily and walked out of the holding bay.

Watching the door close behind him, Turkish said, 'One of his Company's mums sends out chocolate cake. It gets here looking like a homeless person's shat their cardboard box.'

'See, now – Turkish, isn't it?' Colin said. 'The problem is with your basic booth. It promises much that it can't deliver. We see the booth, we roll up, roll up, roll up. But then where are the coconuts to knock off the poles? Or the tasselled curtain and the beaded lamp for the passing through of the silver to cross the palm? Or the—'

'Jesus, fuck and Mary,' Turkish muttered, gesturing for me to hand over my passport.

'I don't look very pretty,' I warned him.

'You're not wrong.'

'It was taken in Woolworths.'

'No surprise they went into liquidation.'

When he had checked us all in he said to make ourselves at home during the short wait for the Hercules. 'Give yourselves some arse ache sitting on the benches, watch the plasma screen, drink the water.'

Spoons, Phil, Colin and Ian settled in front of the TV. Turkish waved me over. 'Hey – have a look at *this* photo.' He stood to take his wallet from his pocket. 'Beautiful, isn't she? That's my baby girl.' She was beautiful. A tumble of black hair, ski-slope nose, perfect teeth. 'Ferah. We knew each other through our families back home from when we were three or four. She was the love of my life – she got all my sweets. In our teens we were lovey-doveys, but nothing full on: you wouldn't even *think* about it with her father. She went to study in Switzerland and I went to do my army service. We lost contact. Five years later, I'm in Paris at a rock concert taking photos backstage – I know the lead singer – and we have this thing going where I put the photos straight through a PC to project them behind the band for the audience to see themselves; usually looking cunted. On this one photo, I suddenly saw her. in the second row: Ferah. When the band came off in the break I'm literally screaming at my mate to make an announcement for her to come backstage. He gets straight back on the mic: "Ferah, can you hear me? Surprise, surprise." She comes backstage. And now we're engaged.'

He looked up as a call came from the door to the holding bay that the Hercules was ready for boarding. He gave the thumbs-up, kissed the photo and put it back in his wallet.

Colin, tottering to his feet, called over. 'Iestyn, would you say you've enjoyed your tête-à-tête with that young man?'

'I have. He told me a lovely, romantic story.'

'Would it be true, then, to say that Turkish has been a Delight?'

'Jesus, fuck and Mary!'

On the Hercules, Colin dipped his fingers in the steel-bowl-in-the-wall *pissoir* and made the sign of the cross over us. We blamed his blaspheming for the three and a half hours of hurrying up and waiting at Kabul airport.

Apache helicopters flew low over robed figures, crouched on a hill. I couldn't work out if the windows in a nearby building had been vinegar-buffed or blown in. A vehicle like an armoured combine harvester lumbered past.

The blond Para from Brize Norton, no longer shivering, invited me to play cards. The Paras were waiting for helicopter transport out into the desert.

I asked him what the vehicle was.

'American. Mobility Airmen.'

'And it's for?'

'Aid in combat. Lots of shit, not so many giggles.'

I sat down opposite him. Over his shoulder I could see trucks dropping off and picking up in front of a row of huts that looked like old privies. He dealt.

Hunched shoulders. Very little talk. Careful of reflections in the eyes. When Rupert nudged my elbow and whispered that our transport was there at long last, I gave my remaining cards to a fighter pilot, who had been sitting watching the game.

'These last three cards are a completely new one on me,' I whispered to him.

The cards being Mr, Mrs and Miss Stitches, the sailmaker, his wife and daughter.

Sitting opposite Phil and Colin in the blaringly hot Snatch Land Rover, I tried to think cooling thoughts. To my left, Rupert stood looking up and out at the centre of the vehicle, like a human periscope. Peering up his legs I watched him wind his scarf tightly around his nose and mouth. 'Room in this Snatch,' he shouted. He called down into the vehicle, 'Apologies, gents. Incoming journalist.'

The back doors of the vehicle opened to a man in his forties breathing hard. '*Occidental Emergings Seen.*'

'Oxey who?' I asked.

'*Occidental Emergings Seen.* Freelance political commentator. Extensively syndicated.'

There was condensation on his bifocals and sweat had collected in a gully below each cheek. Beneath his body armour he wore a blue woollen suit.

'Help you, fella?' Colin said.

'Yes. Didn't know quite what to pack, so may have overdone it.'

Oxey was unapologetic when we ended up either sitting on or wedged in among his stretch-fabric cases, hessian rucksack and black valise. Phil caught my eye and pointed to Oxey's feet. Sandals. Toenails the colour of nicotine-ravaged cornicing. Giving off a whiff of under-floorboard mouse corpse.

'Do we know if it's far to the base?' Phil wondered, pointedly, as we headed for a main road.

Oxey gave a dictaphone a once-over with a virtually extinct baby wipe. 'The plane touched down amid a barrage of explosions. What turned out to be a stone. I at first thought was a grenade. I had grabbed it, intending to chuck it where it could do no harm.'

'You were just in a rocket attack here?' I interrupted, afraid. 'When exactly?' I peered up at Rupert. 'Are we in danger?' With a slight frown Rupert shook his head at me.

'Perhaps that might have happened yesterday,' Oxey admitted.

'Where were you yesterday?'

'Er… at home in Sunderland.'

Giving a 'What-can-you-do?' shrug he continued to talk to the dictaphone. 'Under the stone there turned out to be one of the terrifying and notorious camel spiders of urban myth. Mine attacked me in what was anything but an urbanely mythical way. I simply held it as one would a crab – wasn't going to put up with its solifugid sauciness – till it had exhausted itself and I could put it humanely back beneath its stone. The soldiers that had gathered around to watch in anxious excitement applauded. In general, I have found the soldiers unexpectedly terribly touching in their thanks and admiration for my coming out here. Quite an orgy of mutual back slapping. I'm now being driven solo by them in some kind of tank. It's hell on earth. Well over a hundred degrees. Pitch black.'

The rest of us looked meaningfully around at each other, then out of the windows at the halogen lights.

We passed a squat block of flats, then turned right toward tent lines. Kabul city was beyond, the Himalayas further still, all seeming to have wilted in the heat.

'On the dystopian way just now I witnessed a culturally unsettling – not to say potentially lethal – exchange between allied forces and what were, in all likelihood, Taliban sympathisers.'

Rupert had thrown some sweets to three little girls who had stopped washing at a pump to run alongside us.

When the Snatch had set us down, Rupert walked ahead a short way across a gravel mound to the front of HQ.

'The base was an industrial site in peacetime,' he said. 'Can't remember which artsy-fartsy minister we had out here who said it had clearly once resembled Willy Wonka's gaff.'

'Might it have been Tessa Jowell?' Oxey wondered. He was ferrying his luggage separates back and forth from the Snatch.

I could see what the minister had meant, but thought that the halogen-lit bulk to our left had more of the shrine-and-smokestack feel of Battersea Power Station. In either case, the Middle Eastern lapis lazuli and onyx had been seen off by the NATO-preferred biscuit and beige.

'I *can* tell you that Mr Blair suffers seriously with dandruff. Actually, please can you not record me? CSE, we're having a bit of a time of it and this diversion is going to be extremely welcome. Probably an impossibility, but I'm going to have to ask you to be rather *hush-hush* when you bed down for the night, as you're in with some lads on their way at sparrow's fart to Bastion. Careless talk may indeed cost lives: one of them is Corporal *Mithering Heights* Stephens.'

'Does he get problematically stir crazy?' Oxey interrupted. 'What kind of atmosphere do you find that engenders?'

'Don't bash bed ends with your kit, CSE,' Rupert advised. 'You'll be all right in that respect – you'll do no more than tickle toes with your tutu.'

'Where am I sleeping?' Oxey asked.

'You're Colonel Brinson's guest,' Rupert said. 'We'll peel you away to him after you've all had some refreshments.'

'I'll need internet access. Or a fax machine? The office will be waiting for my copy.'

Colin muttered, 'The fever pitch of the kids waiting for the next Harry Potter would have been as nothing.'

Phil said, 'Rupert, you're saying those boys leaving first thing would be disturbed by us talking, but can they sleep through the noise of generators roaring and helicopters buzzing over?'

'Out in theatre the sounds of generators, helicopters and so on become, for the most part, white noise. There was a Royal – Royal Marine – down in Bastion this tour: all the noise being made now, but with tanks and mortars thrown in. All of which he could sleep through, but not the sound of wild dogs yapping beyond the wire. Written down for wasting ammunition, shooting over their heads. Couldn't understand why the dogs stayed put – weren't differentiating the reports from his specific rifle from all the other hullabaloo. Might have shot them directly, of course, but we wouldn't want a booty's mindless cruelty to animals being just that one more thing picked up by the *Mirror*.'

Oxey asked, 'What are your thoughts as a commanding officer on that? Are any of those concerned in the *Mirror* exposé posted out here? I should really interview them.'

I imagined that the look on Rupert's face just now would have been similar to that on the Virgin Mary's at a post-crucifixion meet-and-greet.

'Already in the public domain,' Oxey reminded him.

'Then surely demeaning to your journalistic skills to simply rehash it. Attack drill.' Rupert had put a strong stress on the word 'attack'. 'In the event of *incoming*, you'll hear the two-tone alarm. Get straight to hard cover and hide till we're sure the wicked witch is in the oven. Watch what we do and imitate it. Except when we're securing the impact site. Oh, and be more than diligent in your hand washing and disinfecting – we have one hundred and twenty-six Germans down with diarrhoea and vomiting at the moment. And—'

'What are your thoughts on enforced quarantining?'

'… *And we suspect* whatever it is of being airborne, so please don't eat displaced dust. Here's your first opportunity to deny yourselves that very pleasure coming in right now…'

An Apache helicopter was approaching from the north-west.

'Where will that land exactly?' Phil asked, hand over his mouth.

'Other side of the HESCO wall, past the Canadians' billets.'

'And where's our tent?'

'Hard by the Canadians'. Let's take cover in the mess room. Bit of a spread laid on.'

'Will all my kit be safe here?' Oxey asked.

Rupert nodded. 'Marines and Guards don't tend… er… what exactly have you brought out? Oh. Right. Absolutely safe.' He muttered to himself, 'Doubt any Royal or Guardsman would risk the dock for peg bags and hat boxes.'

He led the way up a small flight of stairs, over some decking and inside. Stairs and corridors led every which way. Doors, some lacking handles, were dimly visible.

'Jaundiced gloaming,' Oxey told his dictaphone.

We were now in an area some 75 feet by 25. It was slightly cooler here, but still hotter than I had ever known.

'CSE, your venue is through this door here on the left. And I expect you'll be going with Colonel Brinson and will report on the show?' This to Oxey.

'My thoughts on a comedy show are absolutely not the report expected by my myriad readers.'

Colin suggested giving Oxey an open spot.

'Not my thing. I'm postgrad educated.'

'Don't fret, fella. We'll put you on in the sweet spot: immediately after the interval. Easiest place to be. Not that you'd need it. We've already heard tell how much the soldiers love and admire you and like to give you a good old smacking right up your back.'

Rupert intervened. 'Scoff is through the door to your far right, gym near right, go through that archway to the craft shop.'

Lt Col. Chris Simmons, Catholic chaplain, joined us in the mess – an L-shaped room with a bar along the base of the 'L', sofas and a plasma screen in the upright. The walls were papered in red and white stripes and hung with framed photographs of past HQ postings; the carpet was industrial grey.

'Prefab plebeian meets colonial quaint…'

Between snatches of recording, Oxey ate in that over-dainty way of the morbidly obese pleading underactive thyroid, slow metabolism or panic-state water retention.

Lt Col. Chris helped himself to a sandwich, having looked closely at it first.

'Need to avoid cheese – nightmares,' he said.

He had short, spiked hair, a handsomely rabbity face and a self-assured but also slightly distracted air.

I asked him, 'Do you have a designated chapel on base?'

'I have a room where I take services. That tends to be the case at each camp I visit. And I have open-door; anyone and everyone can come and talk to me.'

'Even the Afghans?' Phil asked.

'Anyone.'

'And do you spend your whole time doing that, out in war zones?'

'No, I teach a course at Sandhurst in the ethics of warfare.'

'Cicero, Saint Augustine. Grotius being the big boy of the subject,' Oxey informed Chris. 'And of course, writ large as a prime example of how not to, you have the Yanks' behaviour over Vietnam.'

While Chris stared, Colin said, 'Someone needs to warn the Pope he's not safe in the Vatican.'

'My mate Harry Richards is at Sandhurst,' I said. 'Do you teach him?'

'Dare I ask how you know Harry?'

'From Aldeburgh holidays. Nobody has ever rigged a boat more pornographically.'

'Aldeburgh... do you know the Dawsons?'

'I know Sue, née Dawson, very well. And I knew her mother.'

'Felicity Dawson was a great friend of Monsignor Gilbey's.' He pursed his lips. 'Such high circles you move in, dear! I feel I should tug a forelock.'

'Just be sure not to hold your surplice in both hands when you go up into the pulpit,' I advised. 'Wisdom from opera-acting class: countesses and royalty hold their dresses in one hand, milk- and chambermaids held theirs in both.'

'Specious speech-mongering. Irrelevant irreverence...'

A game of table tennis was being played in front of the rug shop. The players wore headbands, wristbands, jockstraps and desert boots. On the ground next to them was a tray of orange segments, bananas and energy drinks. They grunted orgasmically with each shot, referring to one another as 'Serena, you're crabby' and 'Venus, you're gopping'.

Sighing, Rupert said, 'Two of my Company. One of whom, when not more actively employed playing ping pong, likes to mouth off to Shadow Defence Secretaries.'

'Sir.'

'What kind of atmosphere did that make for?' Oxey asked. 'I don't remember Colonel Brinson mentioning it. He and I—'

'Really must go and tell Colonel Brinson his guest has arrived.' Walking through an arch, Rupert said, 'And in case anyone hasn't guessed from the attire: these two really could be nothing but Royal Marines.'

I asked, 'Is one called Stacks out here at the moment?'

Serena, holding the ball between finger and thumb, looked over at me. I was careful to keep my eyes on his face: dark eyes, a flat-bridged, fleshy nose and a jaw like a captain of industry. 'Who's asking?'

'His favourite singer of sea songs.'

'Ah.' He nodded. 'I'll tell him. And you...' Oxey immediately stopped murmuring into the dictaphone. 'I heard all that. A *disgrace*, are we? This is entirely suitable attire for one of Her Majesty's finest to be wearing. It's not an insult to the Afghans because we're not *really* the Williams sisters, so wouldn't need to be burka'd up. And we're not some kind of ship's support, we're full-on Commandos.' He looked evilly at Venus. 'When I dictate my report into my prick-taphone later, remind me it's double-u in "wanker".'

Putting a finger to his lips, Rupert unzipped a tent and motioned for us to go inside.

'Home, sweet home,' he mouthed.

Inside smelt of damp nylon, sand and Lynx. I heard breathing, and, once my eyes had adjusted, made out an anaconda-like air conditioning apparatus and two rows of occupied cots fronted by precisely placed pairs of boots. In the cot next to the tent's exit flap, a squaddie was reading by torchlight. He nodded, looked up and down both rows of beds and went back to his book. I pulled my pyjamas out of the side panel in my case and unspooled my sleeping bag. My spare tutu again came in handy for a pillow.

There was similar scurrying and unpacking going on around me. I checked on the squaddie by the exit flap to see if he looked up: a sign that there was too much noise. He didn't. I wrapped myself in a towel to go over to the ablutions.

'I'm not telling you again – Marines only!'

The door to the nearest ablutions opened and Oxey came out onto the steps. A grey stringy towel was thrown out after him. His paisley dressing gown showed a lot of pink mottling. He gestured behind him as he creaked down the stairs. 'Terribly rude.'

Inside, showering, were the Williams sisters and other Marines. Even had civilians been allowed, I couldn't have shamed my jelly bits among such jacked builds. I backed away from the door.

The Serena Marine caught sight of me. 'Lads, it's Stacksy's mate, the artiste. Come and shower with us, darling. Five thousand morale points.'

I fled.

Another make-up case in another hellhole.

Except Afghanistan has a sort of slightly less full-on vibe than Iraq. Like Haydn compared to Mozart. Will the basic set–up be the same: tanks, planes, camels, lack of a Dorothy Perkins?

Colin is no way going to fit on his bunk bed, being so tall. And that must be the Mithering Heights squaddie. Perhaps you can add extra bits of pole and canvas in sections.

Poor Colonel Brinson. Unless he brought the Oxey-Moron situation on himself.

What was the business with the Mirror?

Would the wild dogs disturbing the Marine have had rabies? Wouldn't it have been kinder to shoot them, actually? What was that yodelling song Dad did in his country–and–western sets about a family pet catching rabies? 'Old Yeller'? 'Old Shep'?

No, not 'The Lonely Goatherd'.

Where is Stacks? Has Serena Williams told him I'm here yet? I hope he can take over being in charge of us.

Stop singing 'The Lonely Goatherd' in your head, please.

Maybe the Mirror *business was a court martial?*

Don't think I don't know I'm still singing 'The Lonely Goatherd'…

Friendly fire?

Civilian casualties?

'Iestyn, shh!' Spoons hissed from the next bed.

Did I just yodel aloud?!

The squaddie reading by the far flap was smiling.

Blame the anti-malarial drugs.

Chapter Fifteen

I was shaken awake. 'Soldier, the call to prayer's just been and gone. Wriggle on!'

I wriggled free of my sleeping bag and made malfunctioning robot movements until my hamstring reminded me of its current parlous state. Around me, the CSE turns and crew still slept. The transit lads were fastening final loops on rucksacks and making their way out of the tent – all except the one who had been reading the night before. He was standing grinning at me.

'Mate, nothing personal,' he whispered. 'We have to give a bullshit rise-and-shine call to VIPs. Especially yodelling ones.'

I didn't get much of my planned lie-in, either.

'Knock, knock, CSE,' came a voice from outside the tent. A hand fuddled in for the zip. 'Ian, everyone, sorry to disturb.' It was Rupert. He had his collar fully extended and flattened down this morning, no jacket. 'There's been an incident. Two Italians killed on patrol. Repatriation will seriously delay the planeload we've got incoming en route to Bastion. Any chance you'd do an extra show? We'll need to keep those incoming here all today and overnight with nothing to do. Obviously comms – communications, internet – have gone down.'

'Why does that happen?'

'To prevent the bad news going ahead of itself, or being used for anti-propaganda.'

I'd last been in my tutu so early for a prank audition on the Shopping Channel.

The gym was deserted. I leant my body armour against a bench and stepped carefully onto a cross-trainer, feeling my right hamstring resist. Selecting 7 per cent incline, I checked that nothing could snag my tutu skirt and pushed off, watching CNN on the plasma TV and singing 'The Soldier Tir'd of War's Alarms'. Clanging sounds came from beyond double glass-panelled doors, and three Coldstream Guards appeared at a window.

'Why are you not at the CSE show? Starts in twenty minutes,' I shouted, holding the cross-trainer handles more tightly. Falling off in front of these three would be mortifying.

One said, 'Lads, let's get showers and have a look.' He had a mean air about him, dark brown hair in a crimped parting and winged cheekbones. As they filed past, he stopped alongside me. 'You'll strain your Achilles tendon jogging with that weird stance. Lean into the resistance, not away from it. Let your abdominals take the strain.'

'I might, if I ever knew I had any.'

I warmed up at the back of the venue, the Toucan Bar, in shade between the fire exit doors and a wooden sign:

CAMP SOUTER

ALERT LEVEL: AMBER

Facing me was HQ, whose upper floor formed a covered walkway leading to the Willy Wonka factory, then to the open desert. To the right of HQ were parked four Snatch Land Rovers.

I started barre, monitoring how nicely my gammy hamstring was playing: the pain was a little less severe.

'All right, lads?' Two squaddies were walking in my direction from HQ.

'Lad, my fairy princess?' one of them shouted back. 'Lad?!'

I fell forward. 'Stacks?'

'Better.' He broke into a trot.

'Why didn't you let me know you'd be out here?'

'What do you want: our names down as "attending" on the Taliban's Facebook events page? The MOD would love that.'

There were smudges of oil on his face.

'Just been changing a tyre on a Snatch,' he explained. 'No, I'm not going to recreate the poster with the oily bare-chested lad carrying the two tyres. Iestyn, this is Rink-Dink, who you met. He said you were pining for me.'

Rink-Dink was the Serena Williams Marine. There was a sifting of what looked like Leichner 84111 Theatrical Blending Powder all over his uniform jacket. I supposed it must actually be sand.

'Just back from R and R and my missus washed my uniform as usual till it shone,' Rink-Dink explained. 'Not clever when the Taliban gets us in their sights.'

I sympathised. 'When I was a boy soprano my mother washed my choir robe in blue whitener. In the light from the west window I glowed like Saint Thérèse and had the Shakers rolling in the aisle.'

Stacks had struck a pose with open arms. 'Formalities: come here and dampen!' He was fiercely hot and sweaty. And clearly far from being on rations.

'Goodness, you're bulgy, Stacks!' I commented.

Letting me go, he said to Rink-Dink, 'This is him, remember, that I told you sang like you wouldn't believe on *Victory*?'

Rink-Dink kissed me on either cheek. 'Can I hear? You owe me for not taking up my offer last night of a back-soaping.'

I sang 'Fly Home, Little Heart':

I know, little heart, how lonely you must be
    So far across the sea, so fly home, little heart, fly home to
me

'Aw! I fucking *love* you,' said Rink-Dink. 'That voice – it's like you're possessed.' He was prodding and kneading my diaphragm. 'The power! You were right, Stacksy.'

Stacks nodded. 'They could hear him right over the Solent in Shanklin.'

'I could feel the vibrations in my face,' said Rink-Dink, 'in my belly and right up my G-spot.' Fluffing my tutu skirt, he added, 'And you're out here now to raise our morale with whatever this—'

'Tiddle-iddle thud in 46 doilies,' Stacks said.

'Stacksy thought you'd have a tricky time doing your act out in Iraq.'

'I believe I went so far as to say I thought it would be a miracle if it didn't die on its arse.' Stacks looked at me. 'Which – and I stand corrected – it didn't. Far from it.'

I said, 'Actually, I watched footage from two of the shows in Iraq. When the camera had been trained on the audiences. As far as at least one in five of the squaddies was concerned, my act did die on its arse. And not only were those squaddies not laughing themselves, but they were looking in total disbelief at their mates whenever *they* laughed.'

Stacks gave a slight chuckle. 'I did think sitting in the crowd I might have to rein a couple of lads in for some of their remarks.'

'Like what?'

'Oh, saying that your arms were in the wrong place in a couple of the ballet moves. Never ask questions when you don't really want the answers, chick.'

'Talking of ballet—' I indicated that I needed to be getting on with some now.

'Two secs,' Rink-Dink said. 'Granddad!' he shouted. He glanced at Stacks. 'That fucking reservist again. Remember, showing off during the official visit? Granddad!'

Granddad was in his late forties; dusty, skeletal, with horned eyebrows.

'What are you doing with that fifty-calibre?'

Granddad said that he was taking it to show the visiting journalist.

'One, you couldn't show the gun like that. It's got the clip missing – where the ammo box is – and it's meant to be set up on a vehicle or on a soft mount. Two, did you miss the brief this morning? Where combat out here is concerned, Weeping-Bedsore doesn't want that Oxey wanker being shown so much as a game of conkers. Put it back.'

Rink-Dink stood, arms folded, watching Granddad take the gun away.

'He's an overexcited bunny around weaponry. Doesn't pay any attention to serial numbers, dates of production. I remind him time and time again: because of what goes into making it, ammunition can only be used within a certain time frame. Nitrocellulose can leak out past the sodium bicarbonate. Saltpetre, sulphur, charcoal can degrade, resulting in ammo failure. And you never want to get into a firefight with rounds stuck in your rifle like a crackhead's turds.'

'Bicarbonate of soda is a law unto itself,' I said. 'I've watched it with lemon juice, with bleach, with white vinegar. I dye white ballet tights in Darjeeling, you see, but I have a white enamel sink.'

'Belay!' Rink-Dink said, as we walked onto the upper decking. 'Can't miss the photo opportunity.'

He took an iPhone out of his trouser pocket and gleefully waved me over to the sign:

CAMP SOUTER

ALERT LEVEL: AMBER

'Stand to the right-hand side of it, so you're covering up the words "Souter", "level" and "amber". Then you'll be standing by a sign that apparently warns of a "Camp Alert".'

He took the photo, grinned down at it and put the iPhone back in his pocket.

Stacks said, 'Jokes aside, it is amber alert out in theatre.' Imposed at the start of Operation Mountain Thrust, which would be the allies' biggest push since the surrender of the Taliban. 'You're keeping a reasonable amount of fear about you at all times, thanks. Body armour?' It was further along the decking. 'Good.'

Rink-Dink asked, 'If we get clearance from Weeping-Bedsore, can you come on patrol with us in your tutu?'

'No, he fucking can't,' said Ian. He was standing at the open fire door.

'Why fucking can't he, whoever you might be? We need a treat after this morning. Colonel Brinson forced us to take that

Oxey out – who wanted to gangbang me in the ablutions last night. I told Weeping-Bedsore I wouldn't feel safe with him in the Snatch around my man-snatch. The lads tried to talk Oxey directly out of coming on patrol with us, and to just write up a report as usual sounding like he had. Promised to tell him what he might have missed.' He spoke in Oxey's Geordie accent. '"Oh, no, boys, couldn't possibly miss the first-hand experience of warfare, let alone the privilege of witnessing such in-banter as would be bound to be in-bantered." We kindly included him in the packed scoff run to take with us. He was made up to get his very own cling-film parcel from the cookhouse. Much bigger than the rest of ours. A whole catering roll of cling film wrapped as tight as no Para *ever*'s arsehole. Only, when he finally got inside it, he found he'd got an oven glove, a chicken's foot and a box of plasters. Dutchy had a go at him, for making off with cookhouse issue, telling him that could lead to a court martial.' He chortled. 'Close to tears, the silly cunt.'

'Oh…' I began.

'What? Don't tell me you feel sorry for the oozing nonce?' He looked at Ian for support. 'You've met him; am I not right?'

Ian said, 'Leave me out of it. I'm just doing my ballerina spot check here. How's the leg, Iestyn?'

'So-so.' I grabbed at my hamstring and felt the unnatural crowding of the muscle. 'But as Fonteyn said, "If you can stand up, you can improvise something."'

'I'll be right by the bar in case you run out of ideas and need a carry,' Ian assured me. Glancing from me to Rink-Dink he added, 'Can't say who I'm more worried about leading who astray out here,' and went back inside.

'I noticed you were being a bit careful with your leg,' Stacks said.

'Tore my hamstring so seriously my physio wants to lecture-demonstrate it at Twickenham.'

'What treatment are you having?'

'Voltarol gel four times a day, hillwalking, stretching. My mother keeps trying to make me go for services at her Healing

Lodge. She's been in one of her trances. Says my hamstring was hamstrung by a minor demon.'

Rink-Dink said, 'I can offer you a far lovelier service. I'm known for my magic hands. Happy *opening*, never mind ending. Let me lay them on for you…'

I was mesmerized.

Clicking his fingers at me Stacks said, 'Don't you need to be getting on with some of your usual father of twins… *pas de deux*?'

I asked Rink-Dink what I would have seen out on patrol, meanwhile checking that the line across my shoulders was appropriate for an Imperial Russian ballerina of a certain age dancing *Sleeping Beauty*.

'Hopefully, nothing more than the Marines showing a presence. We'd rather not have contact with the enemy. That shows we're not scaring them enough. We'd just be out in the villages talking to the farmers.' He gestured at my armpit. 'Are you meaning to go for the French-tart look?'

'Shit – haven't shaved since I tore my hamstring. What on earth would Margot say?' I flattened my tutu skirt against my belly and made for the steps down off the decking.

'Belay again, you in the fluffy outfit. I've got some disposables.' Rink-Dink opened his kitbag.

'I've never seen bullets up close,' I said. They looked like metal suppositories.

He delved through the remains of some rations in a brown grocer's bag, wet wipes, water, lots of pairs of socks. Folded on top of the socks was a letter.

Dear Serving Serviceman,

I hope this finds you as well as can be expected with the predicament that you find yourself in, having made your specific career choice. I hope you're managing to keep yourself safely this side of the monstrous anger of the guns, as the late great Wilfred Owen so aptly put it.

Just to tell you a little bit about myself, in case you

decide to write back to me and we become pen-pals or something. I won't of course be offended if you don't. I'm called Eileen May Potter, named after my two grandmothers, Eileen and May. I'm twenty-seven, petite with mousy hair, and I live in Farnham in Surrey and work for the local council in its administrative department.

Just now I'm perhaps overstretched with my various outside commitments – such as collecting for various charities (so many, I have to be careful not to confuse my various tins) and being a Talking Newspaper for the blind. Last Sunday it was my turn to cook for the homeless. I have to, between you and me, resist the temptation to give second helpings to those diners that I can see are wearing a *Big Issue* seller fob on a chain. My grandmother used to tell me about the moral debate pertaining to the amputee ex-serviceman selling pencils outside the library in Acton just after the war. Some library users just gave him money and wouldn't take a pencil, saying then he would have more to sell. My grandmother always took one, saying that taking one made him a businessman, not taking one made him a beggar. I think of *Big Issue* sellers as businessmen, you see.

Sorry, this is such a long letter on mundane subjects, isn't it? So, I would like to share this meditative thought with you. When any human being dies, especially if it is a violent death, there are ripples of consequence for every human soul on this physical plane. I think of it being like a candle. A candle has its own light, and by carefully tilting it to avoid spilling the wax it can pass its light on to other candles and cause them also to shine forth. If the candle is snuffed out, we lose not only its light but its potential to pass its light on.

I do hope I've given you something to take with you as you go about your life out there.

God Bless You,

Yours faithfully,
Eileen M. Potter

Rink-Dink said, 'I got bollocked by Weeping-Bedsore for writing back: "Cheers, Eileen, most morale-boosting and uplifting. But next time can we just have you touching yourself so I can have a wank?"'

Next he pulled out of the kitbag a babydoll dress. 'Ruched neckline to show off the pecs,' he explained. 'With matching tights. And these!' *These* were strappy fuchsia mules.

'I hadn't quite believed that Marines brought drag out to theatre,' I said.

From Rink-Dink's look you'd think I'd said I hadn't quite believed they brought out guns and ammunition.

Stacks said, 'We were sent on a shout, he got the transport ship going over the knots, flipped off the back of it wearing all that foxy gear.'

Rink-Dink went on delving. 'Top tip: don't let the enemy have a morale boost clocking you through telescopic sights looking washed out. Use one of these for a quick spritz…' A Garnier eye roll-on. 'Right, here's a blade. And some moisturiser.'

Squeezing moisturiser onto my hand, I asked to hear more about the poppy farmers.

'Same farmers, time after time. The more of a presence we are to them, the less of an opportunity they have to get going with poppy farming for the Taliban. We can do little more than destroy crops if and when we find them, then the Taliban take the loss of their potential earnings out on the farmers. Doubly shit.'

Stacks said, 'And let's just say the Russians didn't get sent packing from Afghanistan with only a tail between so many legs. They have a lot to answer for regarding the demand and supply of raw opium.'

'And we, trying to sort stuff here now,' said Rink-Dink, 'aren't acting on any proper policy from right upstairs.'

'We heard you had something to say to the Shadow Defence Secretary,' I said.

He frowned.

'Rupert told us.'

'Did he now: Weeping-Bedsore? That had nothing to do with the poppies issue. The visiting minister spouted off about Labour cutting defence spending since 'ninety-seven: "Whereas our party has always stood behind you lads in war time—" I pointed out that were no wars being fought just before Labour turfed the Tories out. "Invasions, then." The Gulf conflict and Kosovo weren't actually invasions, I said, more bombing the bejesus out of people. Actually, the last Tory prime minister not to cut defence spending was Churchill, I said. He ignored that. Then had a fervour attack singing the name "Thatcher". I reminded him that before the Falklands kicked off the plan had been to sell HMS *Hermes* to the Indian Navy. And she was the only ship we had capable of carrying Harriers. That would have been a right old balls-up, Mr Shadow Defence Secretary, sir. Not saying that the Falklands was the be-all and end-all back in the day of our military involvement overseas. Just for one other there was the head-fuck that was Bosnia. I didn't actually intend to kick off at the minister. He just didn't have his facts straight. He shut up, everyone else was keeping quiet, I felt like a cunt. Weeping-Bedsore was fucking furious. Can't deck me, obviously, I'm too big. Look.' He flexed. 'So he put me on HQ window-cleaning KP with a cotton bud.'

A squaddie roar came from inside.

'Colin's gone on,' I said.

'Let's leave him to it, Rink-Dink,' said Stacks. 'I spy the look settling on him. It's like a portcullis coming down – and then we'll get him speaking in tongues.'

'Going in the zone,' Rink-Dink said, studying my expression. 'Intrigued about what exactly your act is going to be.'

He and Stacks sidled into the bar, letting out the sound of squaddies baying with laughter. Stacks turned back with a smile. 'Really good to see you again, mate.'

I chose Rupert's lap for the mishap with the body armour: 'Oh, major, you're flanking my rear.' I put Rink-Dink on the naughty step for shouting, 'Fuck's sakes, Ann Widdecombe's let herself go.' The winning warrior was Oxey. He had come to the show with Colonel Brinson after all and the Marines had gleefully bullied him onstage for the audition, then shouted down everyone else so that he won. He was a rabbit in the headlights that becomes emboldened and decides that, actually, it fancies its chances with the oncoming car.

He started out all 'Sorry, I can't – the Highland Fling was never my thing... I really must get back to my dictaphone... Can nobody please mention this in dispatches? I'm up for British Journalism awards in three categories...' – but ended with an attempt at pushing me over, squatting down horrifyingly just above my face for the 'kiss-of-life' gag, and then reviving me with a vicious smack in the face.

Stacks, in the front row, leant forward. 'Touch him again, fucking knobhead, and there'll be parts of you that won't get found for sending home in the pine box.'

Oxey stopped grinning and skipping, put up his hands and walked offstage. Atmosphere had leaked from the room. There were cold, challenging stares. I pulled Rink-Dink up off the naughty step to take over.

He saved me. In more ways than one...

As can be seen on the archive CSE video of that show, midway through the *pas de deux* Rink-Dink leaves me dancing alone, vaults off the back of the stage and into the bar stockroom.

I start my spins as he comes back onto the stage carrying two crates of Heineken. 'In a moment, Madame will halt pirouettes...'

He teeters downstage.

'Madame will run...'

He's now parallel with the spinning me.

'Madame will jump...'

He mouths 'Shit!' and nods in desperation at Stacks to take the topmost crate.

'Marine catches Madame.'

'Fuck!'

'Madame jumps at Marine…'

'Fucking Nora, that catch was touch and go,' said Stacks, as Rink-Dink and I left the Toucan Bar for a fictional extra-private rehearsal. 'The ballerina and that second crate of beers were airborne at precisely the same moment, flying in only slightly different directions.'

Outside, I patted the side of Rink-Dink's face. 'Thank you. Really.'

'Don't thank me, I was only getting those extra beers for when people ran out of stuff to chuck at you. You want your rub-down now?'

The biggest of the Guardsmen was in the gym again. Perhaps he was billeted there? He was doing crunches clutching a weight the circumference of a meat carving dish. I nodded down at him and climbed onto a cross-trainer.

'Enjoy the show?' I asked, adjusting the settings for speed and incline. 'You're too young, but Coldstream Guards have a strong history of theatricals. You used to go onstage in the Royal Opera House production of *Aida* for the "Grand March" in nothing but loin cloths and all-over body make-up. Classic tannoy announcement one day, from the stage-door keeper: "Could all the queens in the place kindly cease and desist from loitering with intent outside the Guards' dressing room clutching make-up pads, wet wipes and Kodak Instamatics?"'

He clearly hadn't recognised me in my civvies. 'I'm trying not to strain my Achilles this session,' I prompted him. 'Leaning into the resistance…'

'Fuck me,' he said. 'That's a transformation and a half from the Christmas fairy outfit.'

I pumped the cross-trainer into motion and tried to look like a die-hard gym bod by nonchalantly watching the TV. After a few seconds I looked down at the Guardsman again. He was giggling so much it had brought on a Kafka's-beetle moment mid-crunch.

'What?'

'You as a *woman* earlier on the cross-trainer, you showed aggression; could have been a contender. But you as *you* on it are a big girl's blouse.'

Walking forcefully, I said, 'Hyde Park a hundred years ago, for some spare change I could have had you.'

'Call from Nicky at CSE,' said Ian, intercepting me on my way back, showered and stretched, to the Toucan Bar. 'Rupert's office. Down here. One of the posh ones.'

There was a door handle.

'Nicky?'

'Hi hon, how was the show?'

'Marine just saved me from a canning-off.'

'Ian says the Marines were trying to get you out on patrol with them. Which wouldn't just be putting you in a potentially lethal situation, but would also blacken CSE's good name with the MOD. Have fun with the Marines, obviously, but only on base. Also, your interview came out in *Full House* magazine. Hon, what made you think it was a theatre trade rag?'

'Its name. And when I referred to it being a theatre trade rag, the interviewer went along with that idea. Why?'

'It's like *Take a Break*.'

My interview, alongside 'I Used Burning Sage Leaves Shamanism to Commit Date Rape', 'My Kitchen Worktops are Possessed by Joan of Arc' and 'Stash of Prizes Stolen from *The Golden Shot* in 1969 turn up in Lisbon Basilica'. I remembered Pam's email; he would certainly prefer the fucking *Beano*.

'But I told them all sorts of things about aspects of creativity.'

'Didn't you just? The only non-completely-fairy-tale bit is about how you came to us through the First Sea Lord and singing, and auditioned for us thinking it was for Officers' Mess at the Hilton. Other than that, we're in Cloud Cuckoo Land.'

Nicky cherry-picked from the article.

"'I was different as a child. My mother remembers me sitting for hours as a chubby toddler listening to Pinky and Perky sing 'I Love Little Pussy' – a folk song that Tchaikovsky used in *Swan Lake* – and complaining that I had lost my figure... Suddenly, one day, in my head a voice said: 'My name is Madame Galina.' I froze. I'd never heard the name before and had no idea why it had come into my head, unbidden like that. Or in that totally accurate Russian accent. Little did I know that my alter ego had just been born."

'Genius, hon!' Nicky commented. Then her tone cooled. 'But alter ego or not, no hanging out unsupervised with Marines.'

Over cans of Fanta outside the Toucan Bar, Rink-Dink denounced the *Full House* article, in Marine-speak, as 'threaders'. 'They always make shit up, journos.'

I nodded in agreement and Stacks turned his pig eye on me. He knew, and I knew that he knew, that the *Full House* journalist hadn't made up any of the shit in my article.

'That's why in KAF we billet journos in the accommodation on the banks of the Emerald Lake,' Rink-Dink continued. 'The cesspool. Whiff off it has them gagging their lack of guts up. But even that couldn't stop them with the fairy tales about how heroic they are coming out to theatre. There was nothing we saw on patrol this morning that Oxey couldn't have sorted single-handed. NATO's involvement in the Middle East, infighting between warlords... you just have to give them a common goal, apparently, like joint responsibility for archaeological projects – he's convinced they could all find Gardens of Babur galore. That's when we started singing "Some cunt's going for a walk, doodah doodah. Some cunt's going—"'

He stopped singing. He and Stacks put their feet together and shoulders back. 'Sir.'

'Excellent show,' said Rupert, shaking my hand. 'And well done, Royal.'

'Sir.'

Rupert looked at Stacks. 'Oxey, apparently, wound up by what you said to him. Threatening, much? No follow-up, please. Actually, should you see him again: damage control. Colonel Brinson's orders as well as mine.' He turned back to me. 'Stacks tells me we have something in common. Both cathedral choristers in our youth.'

'Where were you?'

'Wells. You?'

'Southwark.'

'By any chance under Harry Bramma, the Bechstein Foot Shunter?'

I said, 'I was actually there in the vestry when the Bechstein shunting happened, Rupert. It was Epiphany Sunday. We'd had a revolt in the morning service about the over-rationing of biscuits. Rich Tea. Not a nice custard cream. Camels would certainly turn their noses up at a Rich Tea. And in the service I'd led my side of the trebles to sing faster than Harry was conducting, and Duffy major led his side to sing slower. We beat them to the end of "Blest Pair of Sirens" by a good cacophonous couple of seconds. Dressing us down afterward, Harry got so furious he put his feet against the Bechstein keyboard and shunted it right over the parquet. Directly in its path was Duffy minor. He narrowly escaped being Duffy flat.'

'My word,' said Rupert. 'Many have lied and said that they were in that Southwark vestry on that January Sunday, but I believe that you actually were.'

He was smirking, but not too meanly. 'And talking of which: on patrol this morning, just to be sure: there wasn't an incident?' He took a piece of paper out of his breast pocket and gave it to Rink-Dink. 'When Oxey faxed his copy he left the original in my machine.'

Rink-Dink unfolded the fax. 'Wait for it... blah... blah... blah... fucking *what*? "The mullah was extremely thin. I shall refer to him as Mullah-Lite. *Ha ha ha*." Shoot me now or, better still, shoot him, the fucker. "Mullah-Lite clearly appreciated how informed I was, and that this was both not in a cringing way, and also not as a would-be possessor of his country. Later, during the tense moment when there was the potential for an exchange of fire, I had occasion to recall the earlier comment made in confidence to me that there are certain Marines out here that have quite simply failed ever to make the grade. The one they call Rink-Dink, I suspect, being one such."'

Furiously waving the fax Rink-Dink snapped, 'Sir, the only thing that would ever have got exchanged today were smiley little waves and sweets for the kids. Where is he?'

'Sadly left us, going on to KAF.'

'Then I'll be arranging his billet down there.'

Rupert pointed at my can of Fanta on the wooden rail. 'Royals are having a party. Come along. More interesting fare.'

'The director of CSE has asked me not to hang out unsupervised with Marines.'

He waved that aside with his fingertips. 'Who's going to tell? And your two lads here will be at the party. Shame to disappoint them, surely?'

'I won't be, sir,' Stacks said. 'Off to KAF as soon as the transport gets here.'

'Well, Madame, your invitation stands.' Walking back into the bar Rupert told Stacks to go careful.

'Why the fuck can't you hang out unsupervised with Marines?' Rink-Dink asked. 'Gash!'

I said, 'Stacks himself wouldn't let me go to a Marines' party in Iraq.'

Stacks said, 'It would have turned nasty. They were reservists.'

I asked Rink-Dink: 'Would you guys set any boundaries for behaviour?'

'No.'

'Do you think I would?'

'No.'

The *thwock-thwock* of a helicopter was coming from across the anti-blast wall. Stacks said, 'Remember what I told you, really not safe out here. Reasonable amount of fear. Where's the circus off to next?'

'Kandahar.'

'We'll go to the Green Bean. Your treat. Rink-Dink, keep an eye on him.'

Rink-Dink nodded. 'Right. I'm back indoors. Mank-ridden dust from that helo landing and I'm not wearing my scarf.'

'Really?' I asked.

'Can't risk it,' he answered, pulling the door open and motioning for me to go first. I turned back. Stacks, scarf over his nose and mouth, was already halfway across the decking. 'Germans galore in diarrhoea-and-vomiting quarantine from the infected dust. I'm turning away from anything landing. And armoured cars – unarmoured cars, actually. And I'm starting to include cyclists. Wheelbarrows. Skateboarders. Joggers. Walkers. Afghans sifting through our discarded ammo on the practice site. Beetles. Grass being blown in the wind off the Himalayas.'

Back inside the Toucan Bar now I silently watched Phil and Colin, who were hand over fist selling copies of their respective 'live' DVDs. Rink-Dink put his arm over my shoulder. 'Stacksy'll be fine, mate, really. He's the best infantry you could want.'

Lt Colonel Simmons, chaplain, stood applauding. 'Even Dame Margot and Rudolf wouldn't have gone that far, you two! Nice save, Rink-Dink.'

'Father.'

'I think you might even be somewhat nearer being pardoned by your CO.' He looked carefully at him. 'Door's always open, remember.'

'Thank you, Father.'

Chris said to me, 'Isn't it interesting how your prima ballerina comes across as being a good deal older than you are? As you're no spring chicken yourself she verges on the decrepit.'

'Padre, I'm forty!'

'Really, dear – *in the dusk with a light behind you*? And good to gain such invaluable advice about the proper handling of one's surplice. I've informed the synod.' He shook my hand solemnly. 'Good night and go careful, both.'

Rink-Dink took a sip of Fanta. 'We deserve better than this for our performance. That honking quaffer taking my nice beers off me. In civvy-speak: arsehole wanker.'

He struck a pose with his right instep over his left ankle. 'We could have had another dance at the party.'

'All you need now are the other Two Graces,' I said.

'You saying I've got cellulite? Want to check?'

'You've lost me.'

'Rubens's painting *The Three Graces*,' he explained. 'No airbrushing on the lovely, squidgy bits. I did a Fine Arts foundation at college. My dissertation was on comics; and looking at Robocop and Terminator, I finally twigged that I was wanting to make that much noise and cause that much carnage, so here I am. But don't tell Weeping-Bedsore. Since the *Mirror* printed photos of some of our initiation rites the MOD has gone into PR overdrive. Stacksy's reason for joining up – military might down the generations – would be politically acceptable. My wanting to be Robocop would be a disgrace.' He shook his head in annoyance. 'The nod that leaked the film of the initiation day was seriously failing to make the grade. It was our choice to take part; no one made us do it. Tiddlywinks played with your thumb and forefinger is boring. Why play Battle Stations Torpedo with soap from your hands when you can play it with good old frozen Mars Bars out of elsewhere? And we're Marines, not Loughborough graduates – we don't wrestle wearing singlets and without secretions. It was us bonding.'

Quite different to the way Gib and Sam, members of the Royal Ballet Company, bonded. They interchanged junior soloist girls; phoned in the middle of mains whenever the other was on a first date in case he needed to jettison – No Hope of Entering: Abandon. And, as Gib said: it has to be love when you can tell your best mate he needs a second jockstrap for *Patineurs* because he's been showing a lot of bollock.

I wondered if the Marines' initiation rites might also be a form of sexual display.

'Who's the display for, when it's just us?'

I said I was intrigued, that was all, and added that, having seen what little I had of a Marine's life under commission, I felt they must have carte blanche when it came to letting off steam.

'Iraq last tour we were on foot patrol in a village,' said Rink-Dink, 'going from house to house making sure that the villagers had running water and electricity. It can be a head-fuck waste of time when the insurgents then go in and kill them for accepting help from the Infidel. The children in one house – a boy of about five and a girl of two or three – hadn't been out in the street with all the other children running after us wanting sweets. And in our Company we hand out the sweets, not like the bloody Guards or the Yanks chucking them up in the air, thinking it's funny to watch the kids bundle. Through our interpreter, the parents of these children said there was nothing they needed, so we passed on to the next house, repeated the chat. In the house we'd just left a grenade went off. We went to ground. I saw some of the boys get to actual hard cover, and was thinking of getting there myself. But then I heard screaming coming from the house. I shouldn't have gone back in there, but I couldn't just do nothing, could I? The parents spun me some yarn that they had the grenade for protection from the insurgents and that the five-year-old had just then happened to decide it was a toy and pulled the pin out. Shrapnel had sheared off part of his sister's scalp. I acted completely against incident protocol and picked the child up, ran with her to the helicopter, leaving her parents gawping, and the others fucked for transport. Made the helicopter crew fly straight back to base. Held the child all the way. Medics did what they could for her pain and bandaged her head up; she just screamed. When I ran into the hospital there were VIP visitors from the UK being shown around. I overheard a beardy, northern prick say how disgusting it was that this Iraqi girl would be given a CAT scan immediately, while back home someone with the same clog-cobbler as himself had waited eleven months on the

NHS. I wanted to lamp him one. But you can't even call VIPs out: it would be like having a go at an officer. How could you think that scan was being wasted on that poor kid? Fucking evil.' He gave me a conspiratorial look. 'It took a while, but anyway, I had all that time to wait till my Company was back. I was told that the girl had no permanent brain damage. She'd have a scar, but her hair should cover most of it. Then finally, *finally*, the VIP came out into the compound to have a wizz in a Portaloo. And a funny thing about Portaloos when you're a big lad like I am – for no reason, they can just tip over, door to the ground.'

Chapter Sixteen

'Oh, please – not *her*,' Phil hissed.

Her was an army captain, standing by the security booth in Kandahar airport. She held a sign saying 'CSE' in one hand, a take-away cup and a cookie in the other. She was squat, blonde, her boots were too big and she seemed to be wearing her uniform less as battledress more as a snuggle blanket.

'Captain Moira. I'm your tour liaison here in Kandahar, guys,' she said in Morningside Edinburgh. 'For the second time for two of you.'

'She's anal,' Phil whispered to me. 'She obsesses about curly fries. And on one long, *long* jaunt to a gig told us all about a train falling off some bridge in Scotland.'

'The Tay Bridge disaster,' I whispered back.

'You'll be happy as Larry with her.' Aloud he said, 'You could have bought us all a coffee, Moira.'

'How would I ever know what all of you would want?'

'We'll make you a list for next time.'

'Let's just keep it each fending for himself.' She gestured with the coffee cup and almost jettisoned the cookie. Frowning in concentration, she held the CSE sign in her armpit while she placed the cookie dead centre on the lid of the cup. 'Follow on, please, staying close.'

'Perhaps she could just put us all in a corner and piss round us.'

Our driver was local, dressed in loose, casual clothes and sandals. He was so obsequious loading our luggage, I thought he must be expecting a tip. I put my dollars away when he gave me a Sunday smile for a Thursday joke.

Colin drew my attention to the 'Welcome to Kandahar Airfield' sign. 'Clearly nobody told them that sarcasm's the lowest form of wit, Tippy.'

He had nicknamed me Tippy, short for Tippy- or not Tippy-Toes.

Looking across the vast grid of roads lined with tents and Scandinavian- style primrose yellow huts, Colin commented that the airport was too small to serve a base of that size.

'Kandahar council didn't build the base, Col,' Spoons said.

Moira asked, 'Are you needing me to escort you to scoff tomorrow morning?'

The bus had pulled up outside one of a row of yellow huts.

'I know where the scoff tent is,' Ian said. 'We'll manage.'

'Anyone wanting to go to the venue to do their practice, I'll escort you from here at eleven hundred hours.'

'Please. I need to check the stage surface,' I said.

'I could make eleven fifteen hundred hours,' Phil said.

'Phil, thank you, eleven hundred hours.'

Doors at either end of our Kandahar VIP accommodation hut faced toilet facilities and ablutions; off the corridor running between were six rooms painted military magnolia, each containing eight single beds. The lighting was either medical procedural or nocturnal zoo exhibit. The area warden had his office in our hut. For politeness's sake I thought I should make myself known.

The warden, blond with a jaw shaped like a corner house, looked somewhere between not at all and vaguely pleased. 'Anything I can get you?'

'Gin?'

He nodded, not quite smiling, and went back to his papers. 'Ice and a slice?'

Phil was watching *Heroes* on his mini DVD player, Ian was shaving, Spoons was asleep and Colin was doing press-ups. I hoped we could have the light off soon.

I unpacked, hung up my tutu and read my book while in a hamstring stretch: feet up wall, bum by skirting.

It was a real bed! I might get more than three and a half hours' sleep. The mattress was springy, the sheets clean-smelling and made into hospital corners: under the end of the mattress, then in at the sides. I remembered that Mrs Spinoza, head of housecraft, had been very pleased with my hospital corners; less so with my simple skirt, furious with my flour sifting. I got into bed. The hospital corners had been tucked so tightly it was like wearing cotton callipers. Still, I was sorry to have to untuck them. I was clean, cool and on bed springs. Ian finished shaving and turned out the light. I could just drift off and might get as much as five hours!

Except our room had an air-conditioning unit that at intervals through the night lowed like a menopausal camel.

Breakfast scoff was in the American food tent, a short walk from the accommodation. Ian reminded us to wear our CSE T-shirts for the sake of advertising. There was a far greater potential catchment here in Kandahar than there had been in Kabul.

The heat was menacing.

To a sign warning to keep the inner section of the food tent sealed off as nobody likes flies now, do they, had been added: 'Tell that to Dracula's lackey.' In this inner section were mainly Americans washing and disinfecting their hands before going through to a second area to sign their names in richly embossed ledgers. A bottleneck had formed at the entrance to the seating area.

'Is there a problem, sir?'

The question had been addressed to me. I turned to see an American army captain. Deeply tanned with a hooked nose, his eyes turned up so much at the outside corners they almost merged with his eyebrows. He took off his hat to reveal a classic buzz cut.

'Solo, sir,' he said, shaking my hand. For a moment I thought that he was referring to the fact that the others had gone through the bottleneck leaving me behind. Then I understood.

'Iestyn.'

Solo lifted his chin high, I supposed to remind me of his original question.

'What kind of problem might there be?' I asked in a whatever-it-is-I-didn't-do-it voice.

'Sir, a problem that would need an investigator such as your-self.'

The bottleneck had cleared; Solo and I went together into the eating area. Mist created by the air con hung over the serving hatches and plastic tables; condensation ran down the walls.

'An investigator such as myself?'

'You have "CSE" on your T-shirt, sir.'

'Ah, no. Combined Services Entertainment, not Crime Scene Enablement. The British comedy show.'

'I did wonder why you were looking a little informal.' He grinned and put his hat back on. 'Now, if you want the insider tip: follow me to this counter.'

He handed me a tray and led the way across the black plastic floor. 'Morning, Grace-Anne. Maybelle. Meet my new Britisher buddy.'

'Iestyn.'

Grace-Anne and Maybelle were two middle-aged black women. Both wore nylon smocks and hats. Grace-Anne was tall, with sharp cheekbones and a shrewd expression. Maybelle was shorter and had a hunted air. Both were armed with spatulas, though Maybelle wasn't twirling hers. I doubted she ever did.

In a chivalrous aside, Solo said to me, 'This is where we come for the best service. South Carolinians like me. And y'all should get along fine. You're in the entertainment business, and so are they! Ladies – why no hymn-singing this morning?'

Grace-Anne answered, while Maybelle kept lookout. 'That hoorah of a lieutenant colonel told us to quit it. Advised us it was not conducive.'

'Say, what?'

Maybelle was nodding. 'Not conducive.'

'I wanted to say to him, I did,' said Grace-Anne, 'I wanted to say to him, that hoorah: "I'll tell you what's not conducive, and that's

having things to do with your *aide de camp*, that's what's not conducive."'

She laid her spatula on the counter and furiously primped her
smock pockets. Then, expelling air, she smiled warmly at Solo.
'What are we fixing for you this morning, Captain?'

'Ma'am, may I please have grits, pulled pork, biscuits and
gravy?'

Both woman busied themselves.

I asked, 'What are grits?'

'Something to stay rightly on the ribs,' Maybelle told me. 'Try
some?'

I said that I would, please.

'And you have to have the biscuits,' Solo said.

Reverentially, Maybelle added, 'With Old Time Kentucky
Bacon Milk Gravy.'

From her expression I could see how she would look singing
hymns.

At the table Solo said, 'Might you clear something up for me?
Couldn't say this in front of the ladies, of course – but what does
"bloody hell" mean?'

'It's midway between "goddamn" and "crap".'

I saw that he was making a mental note. Then, 'Can we watch
y'all Britishers' show? Is that allowed? When is it?'

'Two shows today. Three and eight.'

'Sorry I accused you of being an investigator back there. We
had an incident yesterday in the Welfare Tent. It's common talk, so
I can tell you.'

Good. I was on tenterhooks.

He went on. 'One of the New Yorkers – always the Yankees
– was in the Welfare Tent shooting some pool, went back to the
shelves to collect his rifle and the bayonet had gone missing. He
might have somehow lost his bayonet elsewhere, but if the wrong
person did somehow get hold of it – even though our policy is not
to employ local workers as a matter of course – then that might well
prove an issue.'

'Did he find it?'

'Yep, eventually, in back of the shelf.'

'And bayonets are still in use?'

'Mainly, don't let on, for cleaning fingernails. But potentially in combat. Close quarters.'

'How…'

'In training you're taught to twist it going in and while it's in, but it's not the form to twist it on the way out. Technique learnt from the bumblebee and its sting.'

He had to be shitting me. 'I meant "how", as in: how do you get to be at close quarters? Isn't it all shelling and roadside bombs?'

'Some few of my Company are out just now, maybe two hundred miles from here. Three other Southern Carolinians along with them – we all four take our meals from Grace-Anne and Maybelle. And we go to church with them as often as they can talk us into it. Only one of us believes, but we go on account of Grace-Anne's upgraded chapel-day smile and extra helpings.' His eyes seemed to retract into their sockets. 'They're away out there responding to reports of an Afghan kid taking out his uncle's privates for trying it on with him. So they'll be at close range with potential enemy; and so far away from base they'll probably have to sleep where they are. All comes under the heading of peacekeeping.' He smiled suddenly, nodding down at my plate. 'And how are you liking your Southern breakfast? Feel the grits on your ribs?'

Moira arrived so precisely at eleven I suspected that she had waited at the door synchronising her watch to time her knock.

'All settled in now?' she asked, with a disapproving glance at my bed area, hung all around with tutu, tights and ballet shoes, and piled with clothes, spare tutu as pillow, body armour, Voltarol gel and various odds and ends of cream foundation, which I planned to decant into one container.

'What, Moira? I remade the hospital corners, didn't I?'

'Sleep okay?'

'Just need to stop the air-con unit making a ridiculous amount of noise. Not that I ever sleep more than a couple of hours a night out here anyway. Ack ack from over the wire, helicopters phwoaring the whole night, Phil watching *Heroes* on his mini DVD and expleting.'

'You have to resign yourself to sleep deprivation,' said Moira.

'Which can lead to some interesting states of mind. And touch and go which side of the caterpillar's mushroom we're talking: sad-bonkers or happy-bonkers.'

'Any of the others coming with now to check out the venue?'

'Shopping at the TLS.' (The Taliban's Last Stand, where warlords put down their weapons, now an American-run Currys-cum-Primark-cum-Lidl.)

'Can't think why they would go to the TLS. We're going to the Jingly Market tomorrow. Locals bringing in things to sell. Lots of colour and vibrancy.'

There was killing heat now. I pointed beyond the wire to the foothills of the Himalayas, luminous like mauve silk. 'Let's be thankful for the beauty.'

We walked up to the main camp road, past a chapel that was an exact copy of the house that flattened the Wicked Witch of the West in *The Wizard of Oz*. I wondered if it was the chapel where Grace-Anne could sometimes persuade Solo and the three other South Carolinian boys to attend Sunday service.

'Have you read *The Blood Doctor*?' I asked.

'No, who's it by?'

'Barbara Vine. She writes about the Tay Bridge disaster in it.'

'And how on earth would you ever know I know about the Tay Bridge disaster?'

'Phil.'

'How do *you* know about it?'

'My mother. Disasters are her thing.'

She was scowling. 'Phil and his attitude. And his swanning about in his smart clothes out here.'

'Phil's the old-school kind of performer, like the Royal Ballet ballerinas on the trains going across America on tours in the fifties:

lurching around in the toilets on one leg, straightening stocking seams. Phil always presents himself immaculately.' I glanced sideways just then and caught Moira giving me a top-to-toe glance. 'Which, you're thinking, is more than can be said for me.'

'You look most sensibly turned out for a desert environment. Watch for cars!' She pointed admonishingly from me to a British marked vehicle doing 5 miles an hour tops.

'Whoosh!' I said.

'Look both ways, thanks, Mr Sarcasm. Road safety also comes under the heading of keeping a reasonable amount of fear about you at all times.'

Hearing those words pulled me up short.

'Getting to you, am I?' Moira said. 'Did you see that idiot Italian in the jeep? Drove straight through the stop sign. Yes, he very well *may* only have been going at three and three quarter miles an hour, but this is a military compound and he's in a military vehicle – it's not a coast road in some Italian mountain range and he's in a Lamborghini. Good, that American tankie has given him the finger. Hasn't retaliated, either. Doesn't want to get into a road-rage incident with them in that – they'd squash him and his little jeep.' She nodded with satisfaction. 'But now,' she stopped nodding and jabbed at the air, 'will you just look at the people jogging?'

'I saw. Why would they jog in all the mental heat, dust and fumes, when there are running machines in the gym?'

'I *meant* that they should really only jog around the perimeter fence, where there's less danger from being hit by vehicles,' Moira said.

'Again, I say sarcastically: "Whoosh."'

'Pride comes before a fall.'

We climbed some wooden steps to the Boardwalk, a rectangle of duckboards edged with fast-food outlets and bric-a-brac stalls. Moira stood yearning through the doorway of Tim Hortons.

'Canadian,' she said. 'Best coffee and doughnuts – ever! Had some already today, so drag me away, please.'

I did.

American servicemen were playing basketball on a newly tar-macked court.

'Everything else is blatantly unfinished on the base,' I said. 'There's building work going on everywhere, you look on unfinished constructions that even I can tell are designated for use in serious warfare. They've prioritised getting this Boardwalk all kitted out with the doughnuts place and the Pizza Hut and Burger King, and finishing that basketball court?'

Moira gestured around. 'It's because American postings last a year. Their military tries to create a sense of home for its personnel. Road again here, take due care. Home comforts being a priority. The chapel, the basketball court, the Boardwalk. No personnel stationed here would manage to function without the Americans. The British Armed Services, for one, can't afford any extras out here. We only budget for each of our service personnel on base to have the basics. And sometimes even the basics are lacking. There'd be nowhere for us to eat just now without the Americans: our scoff tent won't be finished for a while yet. The Americans share everything. Scoff, ablutions, transport, the gym. Not to mention the venue for your shows.'

I watched a dripping, burnished squaddie make a basket. 'My mother's elderly gay friend, Brian, always said how generous the GIs were. "All your chocolate, your chewing gum, your nylons. And in the doorway of Fortnum's during a blackout they came into their own!"'

The venue was one of three barns standing in a row at right angles to the main camp road. Air-con pipes snaked across the internal walls, a ladder stood in one of the two seating aisles and a CSE flag was draped across two chairs in the front row. There was a wooden partition stage left.

'That's where you walk on and off to do your bit,' Moira said.

Two squaddies looked up, nodded, and went back to laying out metal chairs.

'The stage has to be Mariinsky-size,' I said. 'Proper wood surface. I feel some serious spins coming on.'

Sitting on the edge of the stage was a squaddie with a breeze-block build, eyes too close together like a fruit bat's and hair that looked like black thatch.

'Jam-Jar,' Moira said. 'He's in Welfare.'

'Poor little thing.'

Jam-Jar stood to shake hands with me, unsmiling.

'And what do you do in the army, please?' I asked.

'Airforce. Wings insignia, look, right in front of your eyes on my – though I say it myself – rather impressively large chest. And what do you mean "please"? Just because you're an artiste, can't you just be normal?' He walked away.

Moira called him back. 'The CSE flag needs to be hung over that beam,' she said.

Jam-Jar muttered that his time had been wasted all morning. 'The two privates should really be the ones to put that flag up.' He flung it over one shoulder and bullied the ladder onstage.

'He's the Paras' physical-training instructor,' Moira said, watching him climb the ladder. 'Hence the muscles. Seems to be in a bit of a mood today. Out here, apart from whipping Paras into shape, he does all sorts besides: takes a boxercise class, puts on basketball tournaments, sponsored fun-runs to Kabul. Doesn't have to, not in his remit, just does.'

'Good man.'

Jam-Jar looked down at me and pursed his lips. 'Look,' he called, 'sorry for… hang on.' He finished rigging the flag and came back down the ladder. 'Not usually a moody fucker.' Oh yes he is. 'Shouldn't have kicked off at you like that.'

'What's up?' Moira asked.

'Between you and me, as the only service personnel here, I'd like you to respect my rank a bit more. I'm a corporal, you're a captain I know, but…'

'Is it a bit like scissors, paper, stone?' I asked.

'Ever thought of quitting when you were just getting your nose ahead there?'

After lunch, eaten in the Green Bean Café, Corporal Stephens met the CSE tour between the Apache hangars for an official visit. In his early twenties, he was baby-haired and bow-legged, had a yester-year moustache and wore sandy overalls.

'Afternoon, one and all,' he said, bouncing on his heels as we ranged in front of him. 'Corporal Stephens, 9th Squadron. Call me Craig.'

Phil said to me, 'Now that's a thousand-yard stare.'

'I'm doing the talking in this show, you two. Right then. I'm in the business of killing. And at the moment business is good. Let me introduce you to this rather special piece of kit known as an Apache helicopter. You may have heard of it in terms of its teething problems in the Gulf conflict. Design issues…'

I kept a smile in place, nodded and looked where Craig pointed, all the while thinking of Victoria Wood's *Doctor Who* parody:

DOCTOR: We have to disconnect his bladdermite tubing and neutralise his thermalobes to convert his megaplumifity into negative kreetathones.

ASSISTANT: But, Doctor, we haven't got the ming-mongs!

'So all in all, the main thing', Craig was saying, 'is to keep this baby in tip-top condition, so she's out of here and where she's needed quick smart. Whether it's for supplies, men down, intelligence reports of stuff of interest being sighted on the ground. By which I don't mean the Marine out here known as Smart Bloke One, who always asks to stop the vehicle he's in to take photos of camels shagging.' *My hero*, I thought. 'Last week in the mess they had their version of Guess the Weight of the Cake: Guess How Many Photos of Camels Shagging Smart Bloke One has on his phone. See – as the wisdom goes out here – there is always some honey when, fending off death by starvation, you're forced to eat the darkling beetle.

'Last week we had to extract a guy from an engagement who had gone over on his ankle and, due to the weight of his equipment, couldn't continue. And at the moment we're providing cover out here for Marines. They've been giving back on some hard knocks this tour – hats off to the mad bastards. But in the face of the enemy Marines will go forward and forward again.' I felt a freezing compress on my back, picturing Stacks in a clash with the Taliban. 'And as they're out slogging on and on, often for weeks at a time, they need to know we have their backs with helicopter support. Quick as possible, countermanding a previous intelligence report to tell them after all they really didn't want to be on that particular tack; breaking news of the enemy being sighted too close for comfort to just that very place where they were heading with intent to occupy; and worst instance: when they're coming into contact with the enemy and take casualties from fire or IEDs. Improvised Explosive Devices, for those of you who are now looking blankly at me.' He gave a chilly smile. 'Thank you for listening. And I look forward to seeing your show in Bastion. Just about to escort this baby back there, where she's going to be even more needed than she is here.'

'Oh, now look, Maybelle, it's our fairy princess Cinderella.'

Between shows I had gone across to the Welfare Tent. Grace-Anne and Maybelle were sitting on the bench flanking the whole right side of this vast barn. Opposite them were the Green Bean Café, administration offices and the lecture area, where chairs faced a video screen in standby mode, displaying the American Eagle. To their left were PCs, televisions and gaming consoles; right, a popcorn dispenser, pool tables and table football.

'Come and sit with us awhile, won't you?' Grace-Anne said, patting a spot next to her. They were both in civvies: Grace-Anne in jeans and a blouse with a ruched collar, Maybelle in a calico print summer dress.

Maybelle said, 'Grace-Anne rang her aunt Jessie-Lee...'

Grace-Anne was nodding excitedly. '"Aunt Jessie-Lee," I said, "Aunt Jessie-Lee, would you credit it now, Aunt Jessie-Lee?" I said.

"Would you ever credit it?" I said. "Was there ever a time in your life, Aunt Jessie-Lee, when you thought one day you would have to credit that Maybelle and me – I say me and Maybelle, the pair of us, Grace-Anne Belknap and Maybelle Crichton – have converted a Britisher… well, now I say Britisher, but from all kinds of circus and Russia… *converted a Britisher* to Old Time Kentucky Bacon Milk Gravy?"' She bent forward, clapping her hands. 'I have to thank you for coming out here and doing what I just saw on that stage. I mean, Maybelle and I were just saying – weren't we, Maybelle – "Say, what… ?" There is just nothing I've ever seen quite of your ilk.'

'We're fixing to have another look tonight,' Maybelle said. 'Just to be sure.'

I said how noble it was of them to come out to Afghanistan.

'Our country's at war,' said Grace-Anne.

'And I've noticed that your government likes to have its own citizens working out here,' I said. 'Different in Iraq. Far higher percentage of local workers.'

'The Afghans think it's demeaning to serve other races.'

Maybelle broke a few minutes' comfortable silence with, 'See how he's walking with such striding purpose? He's only headed to the harp corner – that's what my mother, God keep her, always called a corner so recessed and poky all you could do was stick a harp in it – and in that particular harp corner right there is nothing but the book carousel. So what's he setting to do striding down there – read?'

'That there is the lieutenant colonel. The hoorah who said our singing was not conducive. And see her along of him, that's his *aide–de–camp*. And they're having things to do with each other. She clearly had no mother to remind her that desperate is never attractive.'

And Grace-Anne rounded the afternoon off nicely with: 'See this one now, coming out of the logistics office? I hope that she is merely affecting such masculine attributes and it's not something running deeper in her and more troubled. That way she walks –

like there might be something swinging where nothing ought to be there at all *to* swing.'

Jam-Jar's enforced audition at the second show ranks as one of the best ever in 25 years of my performing the *pas–de–deux* skit. He owned the stage as the Warrior, spun me round easily with one palm on my waist, and could jump like a New York City ballerina. Talking of New York, I also had a Botticelli angel of a boy from New Jersey onstage – Stanton – who needed some dealing with. Nothing approaching the level of Oxey, the journalist in Kabul, who Stacks threatened with dismemberment, but getting there. He brought onstage with him a drawing of a cock and balls to display to the crowd. He had made the drawing too small to be visible to anyone beyond the first two rows, and this got him riled. When he jumped he tried to land on my feet. And when he was discarded from the audition, he shouted, 'Fuck you!' and tried to start a chant.

His fellow Americans jeered him, and Captain Solo barked for him to sit the hell down. 'And see me after the show. We're guests in this show, remember, Private.'

After the show, Jam-Jar wasn't pleased that he missed out on being chosen as the winning warrior. 'I was clearly the best – you said so yourself about my jumping. So how the fuck did I come to lose?'

'Because the colonel was a set-up to win, Jam-Jar. Stop scowling, please, it's the CSE archive photo.'

'Bollocks. You're paying a forfeit for that bit of shoddiness. Fizz tomorrow morning—'

'Hardly a forfeit, though I'd rather the sun were over the yardarm.'

'Five am, physical training, not cocktail-hour pink fizzy wine. My circuits class. In your full rig.'

'I'm so not doing that.'

'You so are, chick. We can buddy up.'

Stacks was leaning on the stage partition. I blurted out: 'Brilliant, two muscle boys. For the archive photo we can be Medora carried aloft in the pirates' lair. Yes, we can, thank you. What do the pair of you think you're doing with your tops on – do you not want to end up in the Imperial War Museum?'

Oh, thank fuck, Stacks is here safe!

Out in the main hall Captain Solo was giving Private Stanton a dressing down. Seeing me, he turned Stanton around and gave him a shove.

'Go apologise, Private.'

'Bud, I was just joshing with you, really. I apologise.'

'Really, not a problem at all.'

Stanton made to leave. Solo grabbed him by the scruff. 'Did I dismiss you, Private?'

'Sir, no…'

Solo turned him to face Grace-Anne and Maybelle, who were honing in on him as they daintily but inexorably picked their way along a row of chairs. Grace-Anne did the shouting for both of them.

'Watching your ill manners to our lovely fairy princess Cinderella, I was as angry as our white turkey when he fluffed up his feathers and gobbled. When our white turkey was fluffed up and gobbling: that's how angry I was. I mean, the anger I felt would have inspired our white turkey to fluff himself up, feathers-wise, and to gobble. What's the matter, boy? Cat got your formerly oh-so-loquacious tongue? I mean, is your formerly oh-so-loquacious tongue in the jaws of the cat, sonny? If we were to pry open that cat's jaws, would we find in there your formerly oh-so-loquacious tongue? Well, find your tongue, soldier, for a hymn will now be sung.'

And nobody, including myself, would have dared not join in just then with 'Shall We Gather at the River?'.

Grace-Anne nodded approvingly at Stacks when it was finished. 'You sang that perfectly from memory, sir.'

'Granny's a church organist, ma'am,' Stacks replied. 'One of her favourites. Good to hear it out here.'

Then, as graciously as he had spoken to her, he stood by while she tweaked his cheek.

Walking back to the accommodation with me he commented, 'For his own sake, that Yank's lucky he didn't do an Oxey on you, with those women there. They'd have set about his whatnots with wick trimmers.' He chuckled. 'You do seem to attract random acts of singing.'

Chapter Seventeen

Two women in shorts and vests were waving at me. One was tall and sallow with dark hair pulled back in a ponytail, the other short with bleached rat's tails.

'Here to do Jam-Jar's class?' the taller asked.

I nodded. 'Iestyn.'

'Claire. I was there last night. Jam-Jar pretending he wasn't loving every bit of attention.'

The blonde blew out air. 'I so wanted to put a chair over that Yank's head!' I couldn't place her accent. 'I'm Karin. We're both nurses.'

Ten or so men and women dressed in pyjamas walked out of the gym, one carrying a guitar.

'Class before ours,' said Claire.

The gym interior was ark-like, musty with sweat and body spray, shaking to rock music. Stacks, in PE kit, was standing by a water cooler.

'Cover me, please,' I said to Karin and Claire.

I felt I might be overdoing conspicuous, even for me, in track-suit bottoms over pink tights, CSE T-shirt over the bodice of the tutu, tulle skirt bouncing.

Karin kept close on one side, Claire on the other, and I went and stood behind Stacks.

'It's the Sugababes,' he said, grinning. 'Iestyn, are CSE going over to the Jingly Market this morning?' I nodded. 'Might there be a spare seat on your bus? Serious logistical question and not a euphemism about which way you incline.'

He pointed to some squaddies in vests and shorts on running machines to the left of the room. 'Marines. Notice how none of them are on something as girly as the cross-trainers. We think they're for Paras.'

Opposite the Marines and nearest a wall of mirrors were some

Americans. In pairs they spotted one another on bench presses or played human ping pong with medicine balls.

'Who were the people in pyjamas who just left?' I asked Claire.

'Canadians. They use the studio we're about to go into for yoga to guitar accompaniment.'

'Yoga?'

'They're very into being chilled and holistic. You can never get salad at scoff if the Canadians have done a locust fly-by on it. And in the boys' tents out here, our lot have tits-and-bums posters; the Yanks aren't allowed those, so they have pics of wrestling personalities; the Canadians have one single advert for probiotic yoghurt.'

'Blimey O'Riley,' Jam-Jar called from the main door. 'Wasn't expecting you to go through with this.'

'Look at his calves,' I said.

'What, those chicken legs?' Stacks wondered.

'Ex-pro footballer, actually,' said Claire.

I later found out that Jam-Jar had been a Premier League apprentice, until the night when some of the first-team players had taken him out to the car park and, by way of initiation, ordered him to put his private parts on the bonnet of the next car to drive in. Cue driving in just then when the reserve goalkeeper's wife; who, reversing in frenzied dismay, pranged the chairman's Maserati. Jam-Jar was sacked from the apprenticeship.

And what would the reserve goalkeeper's wife have written on her insurance claim form?

Jam-Jar handed Karin a ghetto blaster. 'Everyone and special guest, let's go inside, please!' She put the ghetto blaster on a shelf.

'Jam-Jar, the Canadians have left their blessing bell up here,' she said.

'Blessing bell?' I asked, giving my hamstring a forewarning knead.

'For before they start their probiotic yogastics,' Jam-Jar answered. 'They ring that bell in all the corners of the room to dispel any negativity. Hang on... pass the bell to me, please, Karin.'

He walked around me four times ringing it. 'Just in case.'

'Fuck off!'

'Ladies present, please.'

I saw that he meant it. I said, 'Not wanting to worry anybody, but I'm getting some dodgy looks from outside.'

Jam-Jar and Stacks looked toward the door. Some of the bench-pressing Americans were staring in. I couldn't see Stanton among them.

'Maybe it's because you're flouting the No-Bare-Arms rule,' said Claire.

Jam-Jar shook his head. 'No offence to our guest's generous proportions intended, but I think that's ignoring a whole other elephant in the room. I'd say it's because he's an affront to their masculine ideals.'

'Before I went out to Iraq to entertain the first time, some of the male duffers of the Aldeburgh Yacht Club said I shouldn't have been booked as "our boys" need nice, straight, normal entertainment.'

'That's what the Yanks get,' Jam-Jar said. 'Morally uplifting, corn-fed comedy nights. Explains why you traumatised that poor chappy last night.' He bent to rearrange some exercise mats. 'Anything kicks off, we'll push Karin forward. She'll take them all on. Poleaxe them with a bite out of the fleshy part just at the back of the knee.' He began bouncing on the spot. 'Warm up, then sparring for those to my left, circuits for the rest.'

I buddied up for sparring with Stacks. Jam-Jar put on 'Eye of the Tiger'.

'See that four-foot-nothing Dutch nurse over there?' he said to me. 'Even she's more aggressive.'

'Are the Yanks still watching?' I asked, trying for more aggression.

'Yes. So how about you give them a slight pause for thought by occasionally hitting your sparring partner's hand?'

He counted down and called time on this first section of the class. Stacks and I moved on to circuit training. I braced my hands behind me on a low bench for triceps curls.

'When you dip you'll get your frock dirty,' Jam-Jar warned.

I tried holding my tutu against my body and doing triceps curls one-handed, and narrowly avoided dumping myself on the floor.

'Try tucking your tutu underneath you against the bench?' Stacks suggested.

I tucked, but as soon as I dipped the tulle bounced free. Jam-Jar said, 'This is going to be the most bizarre form of gym-buddy spotting ever.' He knelt down in front of me, fluffed till he found the undermost layer of tulle and lifted my tutu skirt aloft. 'Anyone thinks of this going in their phone can forget it. Smoother,' he said, as I dipped. 'Don't jerk. Look at your Marine chum. Hate to say it, but: textbook.'

A balding, freckled naval captain opened the studio door and squawked. 'Are you going to let her give you a rub-down afterward, Jam-Jar?'

'She wishes, Chipper,' Jam-Jar shouted back.

'It'll be a welcome change from you doing it yourself every morning – starkers on your bed, being overgenerous with the cocoa butter.'

'Oh, that's…' said Claire, looking sympathetically at Jam-Jar.

'Right, class,' Jam-Jar called. 'Warm down and stretch. I'll give the Canadians their bell back and we'll all meet in the Green Bean for goodies on our esteemed guest.'

'You weren't happy with Jam-Jar being heckled, were you?' I said to Claire.

She shook her head, chewing some flapjack. 'I get a bit bogged down with the boys and their continual sex banter. And Jam-Jar's never in on it. Well, you saw: he's so old-school gentleman, he didn't even want you to swear in front of us.'

'Bit patronising, actually,' Karin said.

'But sweet,' Claire said. 'It's how he's been brought up. And you have to admit, Karin, he's brilliant at organising things. We'd go off our heads with the boredom when nothing's kicking off out here.'

A slam made everyone in the café look up.

'Sorry,' Jam-Jar said, opening the door again and closing it quietly this time. 'Just narked!'

He stomped over to the table. 'Do you know what the Canadians just did?' he asked. 'Weird freaks. I drove over there with their bell and found their yogi or whatever he's called. Took the bell to him in his tent, handed it over, came out. And then I thought I'd remind him about the fun-run to tell his fellow Canadians, you know – include everyone. So I went back in – and there he was with a bottle of water, pouring it over the bell, doing some kind of cleansing ceremony! Am I the unclean or something? The Canadian fuck. Shit – Claire, Karin, ballerina… Sorry.'

Stacks was in a spare seat on the CSE bus. I was next to him, Colin in front of us, Spoons, Ian and Phil nearer the front.

As we drove the terrain opened up and we had a clear view of the Himalayas.

'They do gladden me,' I said.

'Tippy's always the poet,' Colin commented.

'You could call it that,' said Stacks.

'There's the famous Emerald Lake over to your right,' Moira called. 'It stinks particularly badly at this time of year. Sorry.' She looked nervously down the bus at Stacks, as though he might be about to correct her.

'It's the cesspool,' Stacks explained to Colin, who had his head drawn back and an aloof look on his face. 'Guys have been known to swim in it as a dare. Or been forced to as a quite serious punishment. People billeted in those tents over yonder often wake up gagging from the stench. For some unfathomable reason, they're always allocated to journalists. Or touring VIPs such as yourselves, if you piss us off.'

By the near shore of the lake were a toilet with a plastic snowman sitting on it and a mannequin in a chair, holding a fishing rod with its line cast in the sewage. Something caught my eye on the far shore.

'No!' I nudged Stacks. Surely not. Coming out of a tent in the same blue woollen suit, clutching a black valise, retching as he tried to talk into a dictaphone. 'Oxey!'

'Rink-Dink has so ordained,' Stacks said. 'Oh, he's sent you kisses from Kajaki. You're honoured. He's being a moany cunt, so Taff told me. You might just meet Taff. He's one of your lot, so that will definitely involve hymns being sung. Anyway, Rink-Dink had a total cloud on this morning and wouldn't join in with the rest of them teasing the enemy. He'd been trying to have MSN sex last night, and his bird was replying slowly and not including anything like enough mucky detail. His bollocks turned blue with frustration. Then he logged over onto her Facebook page and found that in the twenty or so minutes he'd been trying to get her to type dirty, she'd changed her Facebook profile picture and updated the "Films" and "What I Am Looking For" sections. So he sent her a "You're dumped, bitch" message and logged off. And this morning, the rest of them – knowing the enemy had them in their sights from across the dam – put their chairs dead straight in a row, sat completely still for forty-five minutes, then on a count of three all jumped up, did this' – boosting himself up in the seat, he oompah'd into a Bavarian knee-slapping dance – 'then sat back down again. Rink-Dink wouldn't join in. Still, at least he's making himself useful looking after Stacks Junior for me. Latest is the little boy's doing good, eating well, but he's obviously missing his daddy... ha! Chick, your face.' He was grinning. 'I haven't fathered a bastard on an Afghan woman. Stacks Junior's a dog. With no ears. Used to be a fighting dog. Given us by the local mullah. He'd imposed a curfew on his people so we'd know that anyone out and about after that time had to be up to no good. In return, we helped out with food, water and medicine. He gave us this fighting dog. Little more than a puppy. But already lost his ears fighting. Otherwise healthy. Took a shine to me from the off. Followed me everywhere, slept at the foot of my bed. The mullah thought we'd want to use Stacks Junior for fighting – entertainment – so he gave us two other fighting dogs. Tangy and Asbo – as we renamed him because he was such a little cunt.

We retired all three of them from the ring. Gave them the free run of camp. Fed them, bit of obedience stuff, lots of booty love. Even Asbo calmed down. And lately, when boys have gone on watch on the hill overlooking camp, one or more of the dogs have howled to be let out of the gate to go hang out with them up there. No one sends them, they just want– Oh, look at you now...'

I was welling up. 'Sorry. I had to be carried out of *Bambi*.'

'There may be a tame imam in the market with some blessed barley. They use it to cure crying.'

Colin, looking round at me, said, 'Tears, Tippy? Another tragedy at the castle?' He had a hand to his throat and was reeling back and forth in his seat as though about to faint.

Stacks glanced at Colin's hand, then at me.

I explained, 'I once sang the role of an army captain...'

Stacks and Colin guffawed in unison.

As Captain Petrovich in Tchaikovsky's *Eugene Onegin*, I completely failed the butch-squaddie test. The director said I must stand in a strong position, right leg back. Yes, possibly, like open fourth position – but this was open fourth position to thrust through with an épée, not to prepare for pirouettes *cou-de-pied*. Similarly, when I waltzed, it needed to be with a deadly, strong hand thrusting in the air, not my default swan's wing wafting over my head. And when Lensky offered Onegin the challenge I should grip the hilt of my sword rather than clutch at my throat. I was a Cossack-killing machine, seconding at a fatal duel, not the Dowager Duchess of Didsbury, clutching at her pearls in a fit of the vapours on hearing that her under-footman has knocked up her tweeny-maid.

'Guys. Guys!' Moira was clapping her hands as the bus pulled up at the Jingly Market. 'I have things to do now till setting up for the show later, but I'll send the driver back to take you to scoff at thirteen fifteen. I might or might not be at scoff. Whichever, be ready to be picked up here at thirteen fifteen.'

Phil said, 'Thirteen twenty.'

'Thirteen twenty-five,' said Colin.

'Thirteen fifteen,' said Stacks.

At a turnstile I waited for whoever might be collecting entrance money. A man in a grey short-sleeved shirt and elasticated-waist trousers looked briefly at me and waved me through.

'Why have turnstiles if it's free to get in?' I said, once Stacks was through.

'Just for the ambience, chick.'

He sighed sharply, realising that I had accepted this explanation. 'Crowd control. Security. Or, as you like to call it: warry-mode malarkey.'

He looked about him. 'Thank fuck for the Jingly Market. An oasis in the mind-numbing boredom.'

'Are you not finding the war part of what you do interesting at the moment?'

He firmly, though not aggressively, waved aside two boys selling Christmas-cracker novelties. 'When there's an engagement in progress. There's also the hours on end sitting tight on watch up hillocks. Just now I'm flitting between KAF, Camp Bastion and Kajaki, collecting replacement equipment to send back up north where we're fighting the Taliban for a dam. If we lose that fight, the Taliban could cut off the electricity supply to Kandahar.'

He stopped at a stall. 'Let's buy you a dish-dash.'

I looked around for the stallholder, to ask permission to try it on.

'Is fine, sir.' The stallholder, a row of kiss-curls running from the top of his nose to the tip of his ear, nodded and gestured that I could put the robe over my head.

Some British squaddies stopped to watch.

'Are you all coming to the CSE show?' I asked, once I'd got my head through the neck of the musty-smelling robe.

'Yeah, giving it another go,' said one. He looked furious. 'We all went last night and couldn't understand a fucking word. Thought the sound system must be fucked. Then in the break we found out it was the Norwegian lot's show.'

I said, 'Meet my personal shopper, guys. Dorian Fluffcock.'

They waited for Stacks to roll his eyes before they laughed. Smoothing the front of the dishdasha I said, 'It's too white. I must look like Moby Dick in it.'

'They make them white to reflect the sun,' he said.

'That's a fallacy. All colours have the same sun-reflecting and soaking-up properties.'

'Now who's been at the Discovery Channel?'

'*Reader's Digest.*'

'Not familiar.'

'Magazine/book hybrid. Will show you how to give a tracheotomy with a Bic biro and tell you the Serbo-Croat for antimacassar. Condenses books down into happy endings. *Jane Eyre* in five chapters, with Mr Rochester's severed arm growing back. *Old Curiosity Shop* in four and Little Nell gets better. *Anna Karenina* in six and there's a last-minute platform change.'

'What the fuck? We'll stick with the Norwegians.'

Stacks called after them, 'It's not all bad – he wears a dress!'

The shortest one made a dismissive gesture over his shoulder.

'*Mansfield Park* in none because Fanny Price is a cot death!'

'You'd need a full burka,' Stacks said, looking the stall over. 'Even just performing as a woman. Then you get to travel in luxury in the boots of taxis and in the special cage in buses. If that floats your boat, when you visit me in Manchester I'll get the council to give you your own cage on the Eccles tram.'

'All about men's projection of sin onto women,' I said. 'It also forces nuns into thinking that touching their vaginas for any reason whatever is a mortal wrongdoing, and they end up being gynaecologically challenged.'

'Chick, seriously, how would you know something like that?'

'*Reader's Digest* again. No, really: I've got a gynaecologist mate whose practice is in Dorking. He can do nothing in the face of the Mother Superiors, acting on orders from on high, telling the sisters that they're manifesting an echo of Christ's wounds, and to trust to the Holy Spirit and four more pairs of Vatican-approved camiknickers.'

I eased myself free of the dishdasha and thanked the stallholder. 'Haven't got room in my case, sorry,' I said, automatically.

'He was loving you in it,' Stacks said, quietly, as we walked on. 'Have you heard about "Man Love Thursday"? We have to allow them a day a week to let off gay steam. Kissing each other, touching each other's legs in this weird way they have. You can't pass a tarpaulin anywhere of a Thursday without it undulating, providing shag-cover for an Afghan male-on-male coupling. And a gay couple in the Taliban shot a mosque imam in Helmand because he wouldn't marry them. Imagine me in my bib and tucker, you beside me, in St Clement's, firing off a couple of rounds at the lawful-impediment moment.' He mimed aiming a rifle. '"More tea, vicar?" Ka-boom!'

We were at the biggest of the DVD stalls: 16 trestle tables covered in white plastic laid out in a square. The stallholder crouched in the middle, his dishdasha billowing over a stool.

'There's anything and everything on here, look,' Stacks said. *Sex and the City* with a blurb in Japanese on photocopied inlays, *Bob the Builder* – 'Probably dubbed into Taiwanese!' – as well as some recent cinema releases.

'Careful of those,' he warned. 'They buy them from someone who was sat in the cinema filming the screen. Good from the atmosphere point of view – punters' noise and the occasional chuck of popcorn. Drawback is when whoever filmed it was sat where they can't catch the whole screen properly. I bought *300* and the actors were all cut off at CGI-enhanced chest height.'

'Like with some of the Russian Ballet classics put out on DVD. Weird split screen effect whenever Nureyev's bouffant is breasted by Yevteyeva's swan wing.'

'Is it any wonder the Russians got routed by the Taliban?'

The stallholder gestured down at his display and smiled challengingly, I thought, at me.

'How's your haggling?' Stacks asked.

'Lead me to it. I learnt from the best: my mother's haggle-central. She was posted to Egypt with the WRAF in the early fifties and the habit's never died. And you might expect it on some of the stalls in the Lambeth Walk, but possibly not when it's an electricity bill, second-class stamps or vending machines.'

'I don't like doing it; but they do take the piss with the prices.'

'All's fair, then.'

'Not, seeing as they take such a risk getting here.'

'What risk?'

'The Taliban ambush them on the roads to and from KAF.'

'For pirate DVDs and school of Camden Lock overpriced bric-a-brac shit?'

'Iestyn, come off it,' he said, tersely, moving me away from the stall. 'They kill them for doing stuff for the infidel.'

'What the—?'

I had seen something nasty on the rug stall. A pair of rugs depicting the attacks on the Twin Towers.

'This is some quite startlingly tactless tufting,' I commented.

The stallholder lovingly turned the rugs on their aluminium clothes pegs to face me flat on.

'Thank you,' I said. 'But I've nowhere for them to go. In my bed-sit it's all of five pigeon steps from door to stubbing my toe on the party-wall skirting board.'

'Weirdly, the Yanks love these rugs,' Stacks said, looking back at the stall. 'Rare to have seen one, let alone both. They buy them in bulk.'

Perhaps that was removing the evidence to deny the deed? When Rosa Ponselle's *Carmen* was poorly reviewed, she bought up whole print runs of the *New York Times*.

'Surely they're mocking what started this whole mess, Iraq and here?'

'We're in Iraq because of oil. And because Saddam stopped being useful to the Americans regarding Iran. Afghanistan *is* a mess. Has been for a long time. We try never to play favourites, passing over Russian arms confiscated from the Taliban – just leave the warlords to fight it out with each other. At least then they're not fighting with us.'

'But fighting about what?'

'Ego. War has always been, and always will be, about ego.' He looked past the market stalls to the desert. 'Unless you believe it's one of nature's techniques for culling the humanoid, alongside famine, disease and natural disasters.'

I said, 'War's not something that's naturally occurring.'

'No, some fucker has to start one. And the same basic reason for going to war comes around with the same arsing regularity as does Christmas: ego. Your grass is greener. Your trade routes are faster. Your women are lusher. Your oil deposits are richer. Your god is nuttier. Your government is corrupter. My dick is smaller.'

I said, 'Testosterone has a lot to answer for.'

'Tell that to Boudicca and Joan of Arc – and Amazon wasn't always associated just with overkill buying options for barely last-season Nikes or protein-shake mix. Or, actually, those really good, squidgy pink earplugs. Women have always been in on the warfare game. Maybe less readily, but still in on it. And it's just in our animal nature to fight, right from when we're newborn. The brawling imperative. Same in us as you'll see in kittens, puppies, bear cubs…'

'But then our higher self-control kicks in and stops us behaving totally like animals. As human beings we don't just binge at will, crap where we stand and randomly mount each other.'

He was looking intently at me, I hoped appreciating the insight of what I'd just said. 'So, your point is, we don't as humans binge, crap or go in for random public shagging? Clearly someone's yet to experience a Cheetham Hill kebab shop at the back end of a Saturday.'

Chapter Eighteen

I was in a Portaloo when the incoming warning siren sounded. I pumped alcohol gel on my hands, unlocked the door and looked through the wire.

Before he'd left Kandahar for Kajaki, Stacks had reminded me to keep a reasonable amount of fear about me at all times. 'Body armour, hard cover, all of it. More so than ever in Bastion. Oh, and Ray Latham's Garrison Sergeant Major down there. One of the two hardest Marines of us all. Run if you see a sharkish chill in Ray's eye and a riffle through his moustache. Orders understood? *Reasonable amount of fear.* Right. See you in Bastion, Friday.'

And here I was on Friday in Bastion being unreasonably excited at the sound of an explosion, watching smoke billow. I looked left and saw the shell impact a few hundred yards away on the other side of the runway.

'Class,' I commented.

Behind me I heard a snort, and then a strong, Welsh Valleys accent. 'Class, is it?'

Filling the holding-bay doorway was a Marine with a gap in his front teeth and a tattoo of a sliced pomegranate on his neck. Behind him, people were sliding under tables. I turned to look through the wire again. 'It looked just like it does on the news.'

'The enemy have taken to firing a single shell every Friday, trying for the incoming aircraft. You shouldn't really be standing out in the open watching. We're not talking here about returning to the firework once the blue touch paper has been lit. They might just aim right next time and…'

'Shit, my luggage is still being unloaded from the Hercules!' I was running past him. 'Costumes! Excuse me!'

'Be my guest,' he said, standing aside.

'What the fuck, Iestyn!' Ian shouted, catching sight of me above ground. 'Get under hard cover.'

'I can't,' I called back, running down the hangar. 'My tutu's gone AWOL.'

I found it. It had already been unloaded, safe in its turquoise drawstring laundry bag, still tied to one of Spoons's lighting boxes. I unknotted the ties and got under the nearest table.

When the all-clear sounded the Welsh Marine was taking a bottle of water out of the fridge. Indicating my tutu in its bag now safely over my wrist I said, 'Can't be of use out here if I'm unable to perform. Need the costumes. Wouldn't be believable as a ballerina with no tights and my hairy legs showing.'

He snapped the lid off his bottle and took a sip. 'Even less believable dead or with *no* legs. Welcome to Bastion.'

Overkill much? I thought, watching him walk away.

I felt a rush of guilt that my not getting under hard cover as I should may have put others in danger. I thought back over the incident. No. Nobody but me.

Two more Marines were there to meet CSE. One was medium height with narrow green eyes and a wistful expression. He took off his beret to reveal yeti hair and introduced himself as James Dalkeith. 'And this is Garrison Sergeant Major Ray Latham.'

Ray was central casting for the Victorian circus strongman. Bald, freckled and sand-blown, his moustache immaculate.

'Welcome to Bastion,' said James, leading the way to the transport.

'Fuck me, excuse me, but this is basic,' Colin said.

James looked over the sun-beaten lines of tents and sandbags. Further away were the familiar Scandinavian-style yellow huts. Nearer were some eight-sided semi-circular structures made out of tent fabric, to keep the sun off light aircraft. Nothing was visible on the greasy blue horizon. James said, 'And imagine this place in this heat when the water supplies have failed.'

'Shit me,' Colin said.

'Last year the bottled stuff was rationed and for ablutions they were using whatever they could trap in the folds of the tents.'

We drove past a bare-chested Marine who had set up an iron-

ing board on a flat roof and was nosing a steam iron across a uniform shirt collar. The sleeves hung over the side of the board. The
iron's cord snaked upward and through a window.

'Those sleeves are nowhere near being so sharp you'd cut yourself, Nebbs,' Ray shouted out of the bus window as we drove past.

'Sir!' And Nebbs nosed the iron more assiduously.

During lunch scoff James called me aside and said I must
remember that Ray was Garrison Sergeant Major, and must not be
made an object for ridicule. 'A few things have filtered through.
Colonel McDowall refused to turn up to a show in Iraq to be sub-
jected to your alter ego, apparently. Perhaps you knew?' I didn't.
'Personally, I'd say that officers are fair game. Oh, Lord, listen to me
setting myself up. But my Garrison Sergeant Major is absolutely *not*
fair game.'

I said I understood. 'I learnt my lesson with a Marine first show
ever in Iraq. Stacks, meant to be here?'

James shook his head. 'Can't keep track of them all.'

'And I even more so wouldn't dare with Ray. A few things
have filtered through to me about him.'

'Let's just say that Ray is rather hard of core.'

After scoff we drove with Ray to the venue. It was a huge,
dimly lit hangar with a phalanx of metal lockers at the far end from
the stage. Parked offstage was a Snatch Land Rover hung with camouflage netting.

'Are we liking how theatrical I've made it?' Ray asked. 'Far as
you could get from jerry-built.'

'It's a big old place,' said Colin. 'Let's hope we get a good
crowd.'

'See what's at the back, other side of those lockers?' said Ray.
'It's a bar. Two-cans rule applies tonight to anyone coming to the
show. They can drink, there'll be a crowd.'

Offstage were four chairs set out in a row at a table, leaving
very little clear floor space. I said, 'I hate to put a slight dampener –
but there's no room for me to swing my good leg in the backstage

bit and I'll be visible through the camouflage netting putting my fuchsia knickers on.'

'We'll try the 9th's hangar next door,' Ray said, airily, as though he were always being asked to solve this very problem.

As we retraced our steps to the side door of the hangar I asked, 'How long have you been in the Marines, Ray?'

'Twenty-two years come April.'

'You must have seen a lot of changes.'

'Certain things have lasted alongside me from the eighties: weaponry, techniques of warfare and ABBA.'

'And is this it, you having done your twenty-two years?'

'Well, don't tell the wife, but I've pretty much decided to stay in.'

'You must like it.'

'I've built a life out of it. And there's work to be done.'

'How long do you think a presence will be needed out here?'

'We're in Bastion Two here, and each camp, one and two, took eighteen months to build. There are plans for a Bastion Seven.' Outside, we crossed the gap between the two hangars and he pushed open a door.

There were four members of 9th Squadron in the hangar. Three were looking through drawers in a row of metal filing cabinets; the fourth was putting out mugs by an electric kettle on top of a fridge. 'Tea's nearly up, lads.' It was Craig, Corporal Stephens, who had shown us over the Apache back in Kandahar. He was the first to see Ray. 'Sir! The day boys have fucked about with our kit again. Hidden the posters. We had them sent out specially, sir!'

'Lads. You have a guest, please.'

'Sir, what about the day lads fucking about with our kit?' Craig looked to the others for support.

'Posters are not "kit",' Ray answered. 'You want them up, the day lads don't. Between you and them this daft little manoeuvring game looks set to continue. Iestyn... Iestyn...'

The 9th boys guffawed and Ray chuckled along, his moustache dipping toward his mouth.

'Herc's pulled,' Craig said.

'Fucking... fucking... fucking...' said one of the others. 'Fucking weird.'

Herc was gorgeously muscled, with eyes like dipping chocolate, pinked skin tone and lips like Georgia May Jagger.

'I thought my sex drive had died,' I said, still staring.

'Eat more zinc, love,' he advised. 'Peanut butter.' He held out his hand. 'I'm Herc, and this is Nutter; No Marks, who I can tell is dying to wear your dress; and Craig. Make yourself at home.' He watched as I leant my rucksack against the workbench and found a space for my make-up kit in among precision tools, tubs of screws and gauges that were missing their glass covers. I hung my tutu over the handle of a vice.

Ray said, 'We'll get you back to the venue for your run-through, Iestyn, and bring you back here after tonight's scoff.'

'He's just got here, sir. You can't split him and Herc up just like that.'

'Absence makes the heart grow fonder,' I said, following Ray out of the hangar.

After evening scoff, the main body of the workshop was deserted and I could hear football commentary coming from somewhere beyond the fridge. Next to my make-up bag was a clean mug with a spoon in it, a curtain had been hung above the end of the workbench and the anaconda-like heating pipe now lay with its outlet directly beneath.

'Oh, how sweet. Thank you, guys!' I called.

They loomed on the other side of the fridge.

Herc said, 'It'll get chilly in a bit.'

'What did you have for scoff?' No Marks asked.

'Chicken.'

He nodded, looking as if he was weighing up the pros and cons of this.

'What's over there?' I asked.

'Our den,' Craig said. A structure of wooden slats furnished with two sofas, a coffee table and a leopard-skin rug. In the near left corner was a small TV. 'Bit crowded, but we'll try and find you somewhere to stow yourself. We're all here at the moment. Usually some of us would be over at the internet room, but comms are down.'

'Comms?' I didn't really need reminding.

'Communications. Get cut off whenever there's casualties. There's been an incident with some Marines.'

Fear grabbed at my heart. 'What happened?'

'No word yet. Don't know that they've even brought them into base.'

But surely Stacks wouldn't have been on patrol – he would still be making his way here from Kajaki by helicopter or by Hercules, right?

Nutter was saying, 'I couldn't have been a Marine. Can't swim. Also… fucking… fucking… fucking… cursed my way out of being a Para. When I worked in McDonald's…'

'I worked in McDonald's,' I put in.

'Have any stars?'

'Five.'

'Did you suck arse to get them? Fucking… fucking… we used to play this game during our breaks where we went up on the roof and dropped a little black ball on a parachute off it. The ball on the parachute was called Egbert. I had an accident with him and he ended up getting killed. I thought to myself, fucking… fucking… fucking… can't be a Para now when you've killed poor fucking Egbert. In training… fucking… fucking… No Marks, tell him why you're called No Marks. It's because he once did a whole assault course and came back with no mud on him. He was being a cunt and not running with the rest of us, or we would have spent the whole of the run pushing him over.'

I was remembering Stacks nearly drowning in the water tunnel during his training. Please, any second there he would be leaning against the doorjamb of the hangar wearing his roustabout face.

'Go fetch your mug, mate,' said No Marks. 'Tea's up.'

'Fucking… fucking… fucking… knew a poof like you once,'

Nutter told me, smiling. 'I threatened to kill him. He used to go out with one of my brothers. You should meet them. They're well gay. We were in a club sometime last summer and I could see me brother and this poof in the mirror. And I had to say to the cloakroom attendant: "Don't look now, but can you see that? My brother's kissing another bloke." Then I remembered it was a gay club and left.'

'What the fuck, Nutter?' Craig shouted. 'Mate, sorry – just ignore him.'

I was at a loss, truly. Nutter nudged me. 'Herc performs in gay clubs. His full nickname's Hercule Ease.'

'Oh, here we go. *Stage* name,' Herc insisted.

'For his second job, when he's back home. Fucking… fucking… fucking… he's a male stripper.'

Herc snapped. 'But before as usual everyone starts judging and taking the piss, let's remember I've got out of nine thousand quid's worth of debt stripping.'

'It's what you may do on the side that worries us, Hercy,' Nutter said. 'Fucking… fucking…'

'None of your business.'

'Why would you say that if… fucking… fucking… you were doing nothing more than stripping?'

I sat at a workbench to darn my ballet shoes. I still hadn't threaded the needle after five minutes and I don't know how many choruses of 'Stitch! Stitch! Stitch! In poverty, hunger, and dirt.' I was continually checking the hangar door, willing Stacks to walk through it. He would go to the venue to find me and Ray would tell him I was in here.

'You're making a total mess of that, mate.'

'My singing?'

'Your threading.' Herc crossed to the workbench. 'Give it here. Neatness isn't your thing, is it?' he said, peering at my previous darning. 'And what the fuck?'

He pulled a pot of eye shadow out of the shoe.

I said, 'That's my Ivory in the Clouds Dream Mousse and it was in there to give me what the "How to Darn" web page describes as "The Hard Curve to Facilitate parallel running stitch".'

'Mate, you're in a war zone.'

He threaded the needle and began sewing with the niftiness of a Whitechapel tailor. I was impressed.

'See these?' he gestured to the various badges on his uniform jacket. 'Sewed them all on myself. Check the neatness of these stitches.'

I peered. 'Oh, yes.' There were teeny-tiny stitches immaculately spaced.

'This is the badge I'm most proud of,' he said, tapping the regimental insignia on his shoulder.

'You can't even *see* stitches on that one,' I said.

Herc smirked. 'It's an iron-on.'

No Marks came out of the den. 'How sweet is that?'

'What's up?' Nutter called.

'They're having a bonding moment.'

'Fucking... fuck...'

'Leave you two lovebirds to it. Let's get a photo of you when you're in your frock.'

Herc was flapping my battered left ballet shoe back and forth. 'Mate, this is totally fucked.'

'I never wear new shoes on stage,' I said. 'I did once at Club Kabaret because Madonna was out front, and they were too stiff for my left foot to do fast ups a daisy, downs a buttercup.'

They call it that at the Mariinsky, don't judge me.

'You did your act in front of Madonna?' Herc asked.

'She was in the club; and may or may not have watched me. My one regret ever was not cancelling something in Belfast to do a last-minute Kabaret gig – turned out to be the *Snatch* wrap party. Brad Pitt – and he had Mark Wahlberg with him – went back to the performers' dressing room and everyone compared tattoos.'

'You don't seem the type to have tats.'

'I haven't, but I'd have nicely looked at Brad's and Mark's.'

He looked at me, then quickly back down at his sewing. 'I've just been scouted to go into porn films. Some guy gave me his card after a strip show. I double-checked that his company's advert was on the back of the *Sunday Sport*, like he said. Looks legit. What do you think?'

I said, 'Don't do it. My starting out performing as Madame Galina coincided with someone I know in Suffolk starting out in porn. Same as with you, there was an advert in the *Sunday Sport*. He gave it a try. Could do it. Well, he could when the actresses turned up. Some of them were a bit geographically challenged. One had driven from Slough to Clapham via Northampton, Bristol and Ashford. Like nineteenth-century prima donna Ilma di Murska. She once took what she called a "short cut" to London to sing at Covent Garden, going from Vienna via St Petersburg and Hull. Bizarrely, she walked into Covent Garden stage door right at the half-hour call and sang the performance. The porn actress never made it to Clapham and the filming was cancelled. My mate said it could get like pulling teeth.'

'But think of the money there must be in porn,' Herc said.

I shook my head. 'It's like the money meant to be in my line of work.' Cruise-ship entertainment, gigs in the Seychelles for a Saudi prince, anything for the BBC. 'My mate carried on doing his day job, sheet-metal work, even though he ended up making forty-plus films in six months. Before suffering what he called porn-out. He got so far into porn he fell out the other side into a kind of skewed celibacy. Eventually, he said, only the most random, innocuous things would arouse him: a curve showing through a jacket, for example.' I put on a mock pleading tone. 'Is that really what you want for yourself, Herc? Being hot to frot only with Michael Fish showing a bit of wool-clad biceps, pointing out dodgy fronts over Norfolk?'

Sewing with a vengeance, he said, 'Rein in your wank-bank. I wasn't thinking of going into *gay* porn!'

'Neither was my Suffolk mate, Herc.'

Where is he?

I was all decked out – *please just turn up, Stacks* – and had taken a spare CD out of my rucksack to use as a mirror. The 9th boys were now shadowing the fridge again as I smeared foundation on my forehead. 'This won't take long, lads.'

'We can do a lot better than that for a mirror, mate,' Herc said, unhooking some keys from above the workbench. He walked out of sight behind the den and I heard the clunk of a car door, then an engine starting up. Herc reappeared reversing a Land Rover out into the main body of the hangar. He killed the engine and hopped out. 'You can use a wing mirror, mate. Or sit inside and use the rear-view one.'

'Wing one,' I said, unscrewing the top from the Ivory Matte. 'Can't sit down in this, it squashes the bounce.'

Nutter said, 'Fucking... fucking... fucking... that's something I never expected to know.'

I blotted my lipstick and Craig fetched his camera. 'Get in there, Hercy.'

Herc shucked off the top of his overalls, giving me a whiff of underarm, and I posed with my hand flat on his chest.

'Don't even think about tweaking,' he said.

'Do most muscular, Herc,' Craig said.

Herc heaved into the pose.

'Do something fancy clinging onto him,' Craig said to me. 'Oh, my days!'

He held the camera for No Marks and Nutter to see. Nutter laughed like an out-of-tune trumpet. I said, 'You have to email me one when I get back. I'm going on *Woman's Hour* and they want an evocative photo for the website.'

'Herc, take your pants off.'

Herc was suspicious. 'Why would I need to be on *Woman's Hour*? I'm a bloke. What is it?'

'Magazine programme on Radio 4.'

'Mate, I'm just an ordinary Joe. The magazines I like are *Nuts* and *Loaded*. And whoever knew that radio went all the way up to number four?'

I heard the door to the hangar open.

Oh, please let it be…

'I leave you alone for five minutes and look!' It was Ray.

'Sir!'

Craig swiftly pocketed his camera; Nutters's laugh was cut off mid-blast.

'Sir!' said Herc, hastily pulling up his overalls. 'We were just waiting for the helo to come in.'

'Looks like it, I don't think,' said Ray. 'Oh, calm down, fuck's sake. What law of theatre can you possibly be violating? While on down-time between helo turnarounds, thou shalt not allow thyselves to be groped by drag variety turns? You lot just have a collective guilty conscience.'

'Sir, we heard there was an incident this afternoon,' Nutter said.

Ray nodded. 'Marine patrol hit.'

Which Stacks couldn't have been on, could he?

'One fatality, and the lad next to him shot in the chest. Mission command in the front vehicle's got to be up for a medal. Returned fire, got back to the stricken vehicle and dragged the guys out, chucked in a grenade.'

'Why the grenade?' I asked.

'To deny the vehicle's use to the Taliban.'

Before I could ask anything more, Ian came in. 'Colin's just going on now to start, Iestyn.'

The 9th boys made their way out, passing under Ian's arm one by one as, bemused, he just stood there.

Ray handed me a piece of paper. 'Three names for your act tonight,' he said. I tucked the paper into the top of my tutu. 'Be sure and get the Marine called Taff up, please.'

Stacks's mate?

'Going a bit stir crazy over the incident – gets a bit slap-happy. I need his mind taking off it. Couple of his best mates were in that convoy.'

I waited outside the hangar for my introduction, fear like steel wool wrapping itself ever tighter around my ribcage. I can self-dramatise – no, really?! – and, actually, hoped I might do so now to temper the bleakness. As it had when I was nine and got knocked down. Then, lying under the wheels of the Ford Zephyr, part of my panic and mortification gave way to thoughts of Lindsay Wagner and the possibility of my being the *second* ever Bionic Woman. Similarly, at the height of a serious asthma attack in my thirties, when I was leaning over the sea wall in Aldeburgh at three in the morning staring down at a fish head, almost at a total loss for breath and with no clue how to get myself to a very necessary nebuliser, some part of me was consumptive Mimi dying in the bohemians' garret. But here in Camp Bastion was just my terribly, mundanely real fear for Stacks.

I forced myself to go onstage that night only because – surely? – there was still a possibility that Stacks might have turned up, and was out front watching.

Taff, as set up by Ray, turned out to be the Welsh Marine from the airport when my tutu had gone went AWOL. 'Oh, that's what your dress looks like on, is it? Maybe not for long…'

The other two auditionees were an army Major from Bradford, who mimed having a prosthetic leg, and an RAF officer with hair that had been permed on base, he said, for the shits and giggles. It made him look uncannily like Anne Brontë in the Branwell portrait.

'Don't give me that thousand-yard pout.' Taff had won the audience vote. 'I didn't set you up.'

He grabbed at the microphone. 'Bastard wankers, whoever they were.' This was shouted in the direction of seats occupied by his fellow Royal Marines. During my set I had scanned these seats continually.

'Ray,' I called, forcing an arch smile. 'Taff just called you a wanker.'

Ray appeared at the end of the front row and glared at Taff.

Taff grabbed the microphone again. 'Sir, not you, sir. Course not, sir.'

Ray nodded, winked at me and sat down again.

Taff exhaled and the sound of a whistle came through the gap in his teeth. I put the mic up to his mouth again.

'Do that again to share nicely with everyone.'

He gap-whistled into the mic.

'Play a tune,' I said.

There was a husky bellow of applause for his "My Heart Will Go On".

As ever with the winning warrior, I held the microphone aside and whispered to Taff: 'Just go along with what I'm doing, but play up.'

Back on the microphone I said, 'Now, Taff, don't be nervous. There is a saying: "Some are born to greatness." You're going to have my greatness thrust upon you.' Which was always going to be asking for it.

But even Rink-Dink couldn't have saved me after I'd put in Rhod Gilbert's line during the kiss-of-life gag: 'With Royal Marines doing this, Taff, I find you can give them a choice of end...'

'Ladies and gentlemen,' Colin said, walking back onstage. 'Let's hear it for the one and only – lucky-to-be-in-one-*piece*, at least – Madame Galina!'

Taff, wearing more of my make-up now than I was, yomped to the back of the venue with me in his arms.

'Dirty bugger, him,' said No Marks as we passed him and the 9th boys. The front of my tutu was down to my waist, there was stubble burn across my chest and my poorly hamstring had suffered a setback due to some enforced straddling.

'Cheers, Taff,' I said, between heaves of breath. 'Wait here, please, till Colin signs off for the break.'

'That was a laugh, bud,' he said, shaking my hand. 'Sorry if I thought you'd be a bit more bendy than you really are. And I didn't mean to get lairy. Shit's gone down today.'

As the lights came up Taff mingled with his Company. They huddled, talking in low voices. I put my weight carefully on my right leg.

'How is it?' Ian asked.

'Badly needing some Voltarol and a pummel.'

Ian shielded me from being buffeted in the rush for the two-can beer allowance and I limped to the door of the hangar.

Tutu held against my belly, metal helmet dangling off my wrist, I leant into the rush of air from a landing Apache, hopped cables and pushed open the door to the 9th's hangar. All four Company members were clustered around the fridge, while Herc made their interval tea.

'How fucking gay did that Marine get with you?' Craig asked. 'No offence.'

'My fault,' I said. 'I goaded him. And, thank you, but...' I quoted Mel Brooks as Fred Bronski in *To Be or Not to Be*: '"If it wasn't for Jews, fags, and gypsies, there would be no theatre."'

No Marks said, 'You look a right fucking mess, mate. And you're still limping. We thought the leg-hurt was part of your act.'

'No. I came out here on the tour with it. But exacerbating it was that Marine's fault. I just wonder what he was planning on once he'd managed to get my knees akimbo.'

'Herc can show you.'

'Why aren't you having your free alcohol?' I asked, leaning on the workbench to stretch my calves, praying my hamstring wouldn't kipper on me.

'We've already got them and stashed them,' Craig said. 'Saving them for a dull night.'

'Except Nutter,' said Herc. 'He practically downed his in one over there. *And* he'll expect us to share laters.'

'Wouldn't ask you to share anything, Herc,' Nutter said.

I tugged a wet wipe from its packet and walked over to the parked Land Rover. Looking in the wing mirror I said, 'Now we know whatever happened to Baby Jane.'

For a few seconds Nutter watched me wiping my face clean,

then he asked, 'Not wanting to be rude or anything, mate, but… fucking… do you think you're a bit schiz? We hung out with you right before, right, and you're a bit strange and gay, but… fucking… fucking… nothing like the mental spinning woman.'

I said, 'My own piano teacher didn't recognise me doing Madame Galina.' In the Guildhall Rag Week Revue I'd sung 'The Stately Homes of England' in black tie, and danced *Swan Lake* in feathers and sequins sewn onto, as Stacks had it, 46 doilies. In my piano tutorial next day, Professor Peppin had said she'd enjoyed me in the Noel Coward, but who on earth had the big fat girl been doing the ballet? 'And she wouldn't believe it had been me till I got up and did lame ducks round the grand piano. I go into a zone. I expect Herc does.'

Herc nodded. 'When I'm backstage, or in someone's utility room if it's a private party…'

'Or in the bogs fucking… fucking… fucking… tying an elastic band around your dong-on.'

'I'm bricking it, but then I hear my intro—'

'Gaydies and lezzerons,' Nutter shouted into an imaginary microphone. 'Please welcome the one, the only: Hercule Ease. Hang on: where's your phone? He's only got his fucking act on his fucking phone.'

As we watched, Herc commented, 'The promoter told me to sort a better squaddie costume. Said mine – army official issue – looked fake.'

Ray came into the hangar.

'Your name, Iestyn, is writ large in my good book,' he said. 'What's that you're all glued to?'

'Hercy's strip act,' Nutter answered.

Ray peered down at the phone. 'Tiny things,' he said.

Herc looked up at him with sharp eyes.

'Sir,' he said. 'Sorry, sir, but, sir: as *if*, sir!'

I kept my smile going for as long as it took for the door to 9th Squadron's hangar to swing closed behind me.

No Stacks.

Just that. No Stacks.

The post-show meet and greet formed outside the NAAFI.

'Just so's we understand one another, Iestyn, I wasn't casting aspersions about the size of anyone's manhood,' said Ray. 'By the "tiny things" I meant the phone itself. Gadgets.' He shook his head. 'I can't believe some of the kit these lads hanker for.'

'*All* lads,' said Phil, shaking hands with a military policeman.

'Not this one,' Colin said.

'Nor me,' I said. I was grinning widely, hoping that I was disguising my distracted scanning of faces.

Ray excused himself, saying there were heads to bang together. The Marines concerned flinched to attention and he gave one of them in particular a dressing-down.

Phil said to Colin and me, 'I'm hardly surprised you're not gadget freaks. One of you is practically a pensioner and the other never had anything more high-tech in his hand than the *Innovations* catalogue.'

I said, 'The only time I ever used a PC until about four years ago was at the library to make inter-branch loan requests. Aldeburgh library had no Dorothy L. Sayers. But who's to say, who's to say— '

'You've got your stage voice on,' Phil commented.

I went into the routine, continuing to smile into camera-phone lenses.

'Bach wrote before Mozart or Beethoven,' I said, 'but you wouldn't say their music was better just because it came later. Chaucer wrote before Larkin; Shakespeare before Coward. And there were boys everywhere pre-the-nineties lovingly packing liver into the pipe of their dependable old pull-along Hoover for a bit of fun when Mum and Dad had gone out of a Saturday afternoon. And now what do we have? The Dyson. So over-sucky; as soon as you flick the switch, there's your pecker whizzing around in the turbo-drum.'

Then the nurse walked across to me over the petrol-soaked gravel, arms folded.

Oh God, no...

'It's about the casualties,' she said, gently. 'One of them was your mate, Stacks.'

Chapter Nineteen

'Not Tippy's Marine?' Colin was saying.

I nodded. 'Stacks.'

The nurse said, 'I'm Sarah, duty nurse. I can take you over to the hospital to see him. He's been talking about you. Was actually put out to have missed the show.'

Ray said he would come across with me. As we were crossing a little bridge over a gully he said, 'Penny for them?'

'Nemesis. When I was asked to visit the hospital in Basra, I got all "Never Fear, People's Princess is Here". Now look. What am I meant to say to Stacks? What kind of state will he be in?'

'I expect you'll just listen. And remember, he has an expectation of engagement with the enemy.'

'Public-school boys say the expectation they're going to be sent away makes that easier.'

The hospital was the length of a football pitch. The wards and consulting rooms led from a central tube lit with bare bulbs.

'Spectacular in an eerie way,' I said, as Sarah unzipped first one tent flap then another.

'Ideal for wheelchair races,' Ray said.

Sarah stared at me over the top of slick black bifocals. 'Seeing you in better light, those drawn-on lashes remind me of my first job out of college. The women in the nursing home often had them for bingo nights.'

I said, 'How odd to see such high-tech stuff in a tent out here.'

'Expecting us to be walking around with bottles of chlorophyll, rolls of bandage and oil lamps?' she wondered.

Ray asked, 'How is he?'

'Still shaky,' said Sarah. 'Bored. We're quiet at the moment. Only other inpatient is an Afghan interpreter who got struck with some shrapnel. But he's getting some colour back. Tough as. "Just a scratch, let's not mither."' She turned to me. 'You'll like that, won't you, lovely: hearing that we don't just do "scans" this and "CATs" that and "phosphatise" the other? Good old looking for a flush in the cheeks. You can make yourself useful and affectionately – by which I mean paternally, rather than sluttishly – ruffle his hair. We'll see the signs of him being run down in the falling flakes.'

'He's practically bald,' I said.

From the man under discussion, suddenly: 'I heard that!'

'Stacks, lad. VIP guest.' Sarah ushered Ray and me out into the corridor. 'Put away anything that might lead to the refusal that always offends. Mountain to Mohammed go fish, we brought your favourite drag queen to see you.'

Eyes front... shop front...

Stacks, dressed in uniform, was standing next to a bed. On a bedside locker was a copy of Chris Ryan's *Desert Pursuit.* There were five other beds in the cubicle, all empty.

'Sir,' Stacks greeted Ray. He looked at me, continually tapping his beret against his right thigh, then looked quickly away again.

'Sir,' he said, again.

'How are you doing?' Ray asked.

'Raring to get out of here and get on the Tristar. My mattress has started calling to me – with fiancée laid out on it – my bath is calling to me, the Chinese on the corner is calling to me.'

I looked for a bulge of dressing under Stacks's uniform shirt but there was none.

He sat down on his bed. 'I hear Taff was honking. Great lad to have with you in a scrap, but a non-starter in dance shoes.'

Ray shook his head. 'Barged about like Buttercup the giddiest dairy cow.'

'And I hear you're going down in military history, Iestyn, for having charmed the GSM.'

I said, 'You're going to look like Ray when you're that age, Stacks.'

'Bald as a coot?' asked Ray.

'You have the same way of looking like you're going to butt something, but might be persuaded not to.'

Ray and Stacks compared head angles and frowns, and Stacks said, 'He comes out with that kind of thing quite a bit, sir.'

Ray nodded. 'Been noticing that myself: the spiritual dimension he brings to his life. None of the usual cars, clothes and gadgets talk. I quite see how you two came to get along. One from engaging with the enemy, one from twirling on a stage; cup of tea, discussion of library books; one earpiece each listening to *Oklahoma!*' Ray waved his forefinger between us. 'And how exactly do you come to know each other?'

I waited in case Stacks wanted to answer. He nodded at me. 'I sang at the T200 dinner on HMS *Victory* and Stacks was the unwelcoming committee.'

'He has a set of lungs on him you wouldn't believe, sir.'

Ray glanced briefly at my tutu skirt.

'Nothing like that,' Stacks said. 'Best bib and tucker, maximum decorum.'

I said, 'Orders from Sir Alan. Black tie, no talking in front of Her Majesty, not a sniff of eyeliner. Anything untoward the press might have got hold of to be played down.'

'Was there anything?' Ray asked, amused.

'Only a photo of me dancing Sugar Plum with one of my chins displaced.'

'Wish I'd known you at the time, Iestyn. I missed out in the lottery draw to get a place on board for T200.'

'I'll never forget when Louisa and I rounded the corner of the dockyard and there it was: *Victory* all togged out.'

'There *she* was,' Stacks corrected me. 'And as far as I remember it you rounded that corner with a rifle trained on your backside.'

He moved the copy of *Desert Pursuit* a few centimetres, then back to where it had been. A muscle ticked in his left cheek. He looked at me. 'I'm coming back out here after this enforced R and R. I haven't finished with them yet. I don't respect them as an enemy. They're not good soldiers. They're not out in the open as a fighting unit wearing uniforms. They're sneaking around dressed like everyone else. With children kept clearly visible along with them.

And ambushing's not soldierly. I got this' – he waved his hand over his chest – 'in one of their typical gutless ambushes. It's what our guys fear the most: not going out guns blazing. I didn't even get my weapon to my shoulder. Neither did Smithy next to me.' His eyes shone suddenly. He swallowed. 'And my boys will still be out here.

'My mum was actually made up when I passed training. It'll be hard for her when I come back out here because this will have brought the reality home to her that it's not all parades, massed bands playing "All the Nice Girls Love a Sailor" and doing assault courses on *Blue Peter*. But at least she gets to meet me alive off the plane, and not a box of body parts draped in a flag. Smithy's mum's not getting him back. For his sake, I can't have finished yet. Sorry, sir,' he looked at Ray, 'dragging something personal into it.'

'Royal,' Ray said, clipping the word with meaning.

Stacks and I hugged, the plaster beneath his shirt rasping. The debilitating injury to my hamstring now seemed like nothing. He unzipped the cubicle flap and held it for Ray and me to pass through. Sarah was scooting herself back and forth across the floor in a chair on wheels. She saw us and jammed to a heel-stop. 'Have you—?' she mimed to me.

I ruffled what there was of Stacks's hair.

'What?' he asked, bemused.

'No flakes,' said Sarah. 'Means we don't have to worry about you being too run down to fly.'

Stacks hugged me again. 'Cheers so much for coming to see me, chick. Keep twirling.'

'And you, keep killing.'

Taff unzipped the tent flap and squeezed through. He said 'Sir' to Ray and then shook his head at Stacks.

'Heard you were malingering in here, titch. What kind of fucktard are you getting shot? Massive rocket attack they put on in Kajaki to welcome you. Your animal porn still in your kitbag. Weren't wearing your body armour. Totally missed you. And then look. Doing your Noddy and Big Ears act driving along in the open with Smithy, rest him, and they score a direct hit.'

'It's called active duty, Taff. You should get your feet from under a desk and try it.'

Taff grinned, looking at Ray. 'Even the rocket that came down right in the middle of us missed him, sir. Not a scratch. Looked fucking hilarious the way he skipped sideways like a penguin having a fit, mind.'

I asked, 'What's it like when the rockets are properly close?'

'They're like wasps whizzing past you,' Stacks said. 'You either end up in a panic or in a giggling fit. One of the rockets in the Kajaki engagement went into the wall of the position, turned the mud into lava, along with half the CO's face. There's nothing you can do other than get down and hope they miss you.'

Taff gave me an arch look. 'Is this you doing research for when you pretend the one at the airheads was closer than it was? If I happen to come and see you perform back home and hear you talking about it taking your right hip off or something, I'll know the truth and call you out from up in the balcony.' He turned to Stacks. 'You missed it,' he giggled, letting air escape through the gap in his front teeth. 'Incoming at the airheads. First he's outside watching it like it's on TV; then he's refusing to get under hard cover because he can't find his frock. Skipping down the hangar bleating how his tutu's gone AWOL!'

Stacks was white and staring. 'The fuck, Iestyn!'

'Blood pressure,' Sarah warned.

'The *fuck*?!' Stacks jabbed at my chest. Taff watched him. 'What did I say about a reasonable amount of fear? *What did I say?* And you ignore protocol when an alarm goes off?' He stopped jabbing and stared down at me. 'Sir, when I'm let out of here, permission to go back to my billet via the cookhouse with Taff and whoever else I can muster?'

'Granted,' Ray said, after a moment's thought. 'Just don't let Taff lick any spoons.'

Taff started to say something, but clearly thought better of it.

'You're really in fucking trouble this time.' Stacks turned to walk back to his room. Taff went with him.

'Stacks?'

He ignored me.

Sarah came with Ray and me as far as the front of the hospital. I said I couldn't believe I'd just told Stacks to keep killing.

'He's not out here to do a milk round, love.' She gave me a package. 'We noticed you've been obviously in a lot of pain with your leg post-Taff. I shouldn't do this really without a doctor's say-so and a script and all that, but here – for the madness of that act, *you* can have a suppository!'

'Iestyn.' It was Stacks, holding the tent flap aside. He tipped a finger in my direction. 'Save me a seat at the front of the Tristar and you might be off the hook… ish.'

The next morning, after scoff, we weren't allowed back into the CSE tent. An incident, Ray said. 'Security breach of some sort. We need you to stay right away from the area.'

As we went, Colin stuck his fingers in his ears and shouted, 'Bang!'

When Ray gave us the all-clear to go back to the tent I found my bed looking like Christmas had come early, though not in a good way. All my belongings – spare-tutu pillow, bedding roll, clothes, dressing gown, towel, flip flops, sandals, shoes, toiletries, make-up, books, notepad – had been wrapped in cling film.

'What the blimey-O-Riley, Iestyn?' Phil wondered.

'Royal Marine practical joke,' I said, starting to unwrap the cling-film parcels. 'Let's just hope there isn't a chicken's foot in one of them.'

The unwrapping took me an hour all told. In one of the parcels was a note:

> You'll keep a reasonable amount of fucking fear from here on in, won't you, princess???!!! Love ya really, Stacks.
>
> PS Don't forget my seat on the Trident – oops – Tristar. xxx

Chapter Twenty

Ray came with the news that the Tristar was AWOL – he didn't know where – due to an issue with security clearance. We later heard that it was in Belfast, Hanover, Istanbul, the Falklands, definitely Hanover, Brisbane, Crete, Hanover (how many more times?), Marbella, Toronto, Sicily, Hanover – stop saying that or I'll fucking bite you! – and the Seychelles.

Wherever it might have been, it was not due in Kandahar until Saturday. We would be stuck in Afghanistan for at least two more days. Phil and Colin would both have to cancel sets at Jongleurs, Spoons an arena show, me a return to Bocking for the elected Dean's church flowers festival. Except that the President of Estonia finished an official visit that afternoon in Bastion and refused to wait for the Tristar; he commandeered a Hercules to take him to Qatar, where he would board a commercial flight. Our people spoke to his people and we went along for the ride.

I was so grateful, I offered the President a pack of the custard creams that I'd inevitably saved from a bag ration. 'Brilliant you were able to pull rank like this, your... er... President. Oh, you're more than welcome. They're wasted on the camels.'

I tried to get Stacks on the Hercules flight. 'But he's been *shot*,' I insisted to the check-in official. He was short, stern and had hair the colour of tarnished gold.

'His injury isn't nearly serious enough.' He turned a questioning look on Stacks. 'Not to mention the official protocol needing to be observed.'

'I observed all the protocol. I gave the President of Estonia my spare custard creams – and it's his plane!'

Stacks, resigned, bent to pick up his kitbag. 'Worth a try, chick. Er, no, belay!' He held me by the shoulders. I'd been off to ask the President to pull rank. 'Oh, now – where's a tame imam with the blessed barley when you need it? Seriously, the President couldn't interfere.'

'He can give me back my bloody custard creams. When do you actually ever *hear* about Estonia other than on Eurovision night? You're not well.'

'I'll be fine. Chick, remember, it's what I do. You know what they say about being big enough and ugly enough? First half applies. I'm keeping hold of the bullet they took out of me to have my name engraved on. And when I go out on the pull, the women will flock to my war wound.'

Which, on my advice, he emphasises with lip liner.

There was a while before the flight and tea-making facilities in a side room. Stacks brewed up. 'Sorry, it's bags.'

He had more colour, the livid tint was fading from the whites of his eyes, but he had by no means recovered his swagger. I said, 'Surely there are other things you can do? You're brilliant; you've got a brain in your head. You don't have to be a Marine.'

He held my gaze dead straight. '*Royal* Marine. Are there are a lot of other things you can do? Other than tiddle-tiddle-thud in six dozen doilies, making your flouncy quips or having old seadogs in tears singing naval ditties?'

'No. For better or worse I'm stuck with sequins and "Sea Fever" till I go into Pam's home for Sugar Plum has-beens.'

'It's a living. Mine too. For at least the next thirteen years. And as many that make it that far would tell you, it's after that the real shit starts. Ask Pam about the guys of his age that have tried to reintegrate into society. The ones that saw shouts in Northern Island, the Falklands or the first Gulf conflict. And their plight is the same as it always was, and is set to continue. Literary reference? Quick...'

'Fanny Price's father: *Mansfield Park*. Invalided out of the Marines – sorry, *Royal* Marines. Alcoholic. Unemployed. Best all round that Fanny's adopted by rich relatives. So, then, as they say, it's an ill wind...'

'I can always rely on you, chick. But it's true: when the bed and full board, healthcare and following orders without question comes to an end, we so easily fall through the cracks. There's not so many cardboard boxes these days, of course, cos packaging's been so curtailed. Hare Krishna pad thai noodles alongside Salvation Army chicken soup. Selling the *Big Issue*, rather than the pencils...' He smiled at this reference to Rink-Dink's wank-free do-gooder letter.

The Hercules was ready for boarding.

'Go careful,' Stacks said, binning our polystyrene cups. His hug was engulfing and he smelt of clean clothes and antiseptic. 'Message me as soon as you're back safe.'

At my desk in my St Pancras bedsit I saw that, finally, there was a little green dot by Stacks's name on Facebook chat.

'Stacks!'

'All right, princess?!!!'

'When are they flying you home?'

'Saturday still, all going to plan. How was your trip home?'

'Stupid of Fräulein Gretl, in the Hanover airport sweetie emporium, to display the biscuits in bowls to be sold by weight. With the price hidden *and in a foreign language* on the bottoms. Just asking for me to think they were free samples and royally help myself. She nearly had me arrested.'

'Ha ha ha ha! Trust you. Come to Manchester and see me, remember?'

'Okay. Maybe before you go back out again to Afghanistan – when will that be?'

'Killing starts again mid-June.'

Epilogue

Stacks and I were billed together for a *Seawords* event. Sir Alan West had first heard me sing at *Seawords* in 2004, leading to the gig on *Victory* and the CSE tours of Iraq and Afghanistan. He and Lady Rosie would be at this one.

Stacks suggested places to meet in London for lunch on the day. 'I know the tattoo parlours, or Guilty Pleasures at KOKO and this weird little theatre near Hampstead Heath. There was this girl dressed in a bodice made out of nappy pins and what looked like laminated cabbage. Her act was a bit of dancing, but mainly she had a Speak & Spell rewired to sound-bite about her uncle abusing her.'

'I know the Sue Ryders, the libraries and the crypt of St Dominic's, Haverstock Hill, where they have free string-quartet recitals.'

We compromised and met at the Clink Street Wagamama.

At the Trafalgar Tavern that evening, Stacks was introduced as one of 'Her Majesty's Finest', here to regale the company with one of the great, epic tales of seafaring. He was in full regimental dress.

'Has that been percolating ready-to-wear tonight in the corner of your garage where the cat pisses?' I wondered.

He walked to the lectern. Reaching up to touch his scar raised and lowered his medals, sending out shards of light. He caught my eye, and I knew, but *knew*, that this had been a bit of stage business. Behind him was the painting of Nelson lying fatally wounded. Stacks stared at the company, saluted Sir Alan.

Then he began his great, epic tale of seafaring, 'The Owl and the Pussycat Went to Sea...'

'Splendid, truly splendid,' retired Naval Commander Peter Soames congratulated Stacks. 'And such an honour to have you perform here.'

He turned to me. 'Iestyn, I hear that you've been put in certain people's wills in Aldeburgh to sing at their funerals?'

'I've sung "On Wings of Song" for Ethel Keane and "The Holy City" for Tessa Bartholomew, great ladies of Aldeburgh. And I'm down to sing "Miss Otis Regrets" for Jo Heggarty and Jill Ibb.'

'Can you please put me down along with them – for "Tom Bowling"?'

Which, as it was always requested, I sang that night. On my way back to the table I passed Lady Rosie, Sir Alan's wife, who pulled me to her. 'Remember what I told you last time we were here?'

About being reluctant to go to naval events with her husband, seeing that he and his cronies always end up crying. She pointed at Sir Alan, Stacks and Peter Soames, all of whom were in tears.

'Call the imam. Blessed barley for table nine!' I said, watching Stacks press his thumbs into his eyelids.

'"Tom Bowling" always *kills* me,' he said. 'Even when sung from the *Naughty Tank* in Iraq.' Quietly, he added, 'Iestyn, I'd like to think, if the worst came to the worst, you'd sing that for me.'

I exhaled, feeling my eyes get moist. 'Couldn't tell you the honour. But let's hope I won't ever have to.'

He picked up his wine glass, indicating that I should do the same. 'You can have too much lip, too low cleavage and nearly caused an international incident wanting to confiscate the President of Estonia's custard creams to give back to the camels. But, chick, you're essence.'

High praise in Marine-speak.

As he started his whitebait there were still tears in his eyes. I said, 'What's the quote about the First World War Colonel? "He was, like most military men, really abnormally sensitive."'

'Lawrence of Arabia, *The Seven Pillars of Wisdom*?'

'No. Miss Marple, *The Body in the Library*.'

It's the one time ever I've had the last word with him.

Acknowledgements

Stacks, of course, always in the first line. Best, funniest and truest of mates. Rink-Dink, Pam, Ray, Moira et al, for letting me tell their stories. Stella Beddard, who taught me all the ballet in the foyer if the Royal Opera House. Nicky Ness, AKA Miss, who took the punt of all punts. Lizzie Roper, naturally. Ken Levison, who said he wouldn't, dear boy, dream of interfering with this book... but then did – and so hoorahly.

Lis and Dr Hanne Bewernick for their continued insights into how this all might work. The great, no longer with us, ladies of Aldeburgh: Margaret Catchpole, Mrs Cooney, Ethel Keane and Tessa Bartholomew – for all your cheering as I went. Libby Purves, OBE, for booking me for that Seawords evening in the first place.

Whatever's right with this book is thanks to others. Whatever's wrong with it is down to me.

Patrons

Lady Alex
Saba 'Brownie' Ali
Suelan Allison
Caroline Amer
Lucy Andre
Michelle Andrew
Ghislan Arthur
Jan Arthur
S Ascom
Leonard Bacica
Matt Barnard
Charles Barrett
Adam Basil
Lottie Bedlow
Camilla Belsvik
Lis Bewernick
Astrid Bewernick
Hanne Bewernick
Henry Bonas
John Brassey
Alice Broadribb
Keith Carabine
Fiona Cave
Catia Ciarico
Emma Cooper
Kate Creevey
Ian Crouch
Paula Cunliffe
Scott Stewart Curnow
Herring Bone Design
Romany Diva of Magic
Jeremy Doughton
Antony Dowson
Andy DunfieldPrayero
Janine Edge

Eirwen Edwards
Rania El-Kurdi
Caroline Elsey
Chris Essex-Hill
Sally Evans
Chris Forrest
Louise Gibb
Lamorna Good
Tony Gray
Christopher Green
Russ Haines
Alexander Hall
Richard Harris
JoJo Hatley
Mark Hegarty
Jon Hicks
Lisa Holdsworth
Sophie Holloway
Kalki Hoops
Toby Keane
Tania Kenny
Christian Lee
Sybaris Linderman
Lizzieroper Lizzieroper
Mark Lynch
Cherie Matrix-Holt
Philip McGough
Maggie Morgan
Aldeburgh Music
Seraphina Myers
Carol Neale
Jeremy Nicholas
Spencer O'Driscoll
Adam Oliver
Judith Payne
Stewart Pemberton
David Pickering
Diana Piercy
Polly Rae

Martin Ramsdin
Julius Reed
Felipe Reyes
Sarah Rowland
Louisa Ruthven
Amy Saunders
Lynn Shell
Jeff Short
William Simpson
Phoebe Rose Smith
Peter Snipp
Beverley Snodgrass
Claire Steghart
Black and Tan
Charlotte Tate
Dave Thomson
Louisa Thorp
Joanna Tittykaka
Piers Torday
Duncan Turner
Marilyn Tyzack
Tom Vining
Laurelie Walter
Sandra Wellstead
Julia Whitfield